THE
MIDDLE KINGDOM
RIDE

Two brothers, two motorcycles,

one epic journey around China

COLIN PYLE and RYAN PYLE

Published by G219 Productions Limited

www.G219Productions.com

www.mkride.com

ISBN: 146815981X
ISBN 13: 9781468159813

FIRST EDITION
Designed by Jonathan Hogan
Cover Photograph by Chad Ingraham

Library of Congress Cataloging-in-Publication Data
Pyle, Colin and Pyle, Ryan
The Middle Kingdom Ride: Two brothers, two motorcycles, one epic 18,000 km journey around China / Colin Pyle and Ryan Pyle.
p. cm.
ISBN 978-1468159813
1. China – Description and Travel. Adventure. 2. Transportation. Automotive. Motorcycle.
China. I. Title

This book is dedicated to our wives,
Emma and Jasmine,
for supporting our insane ideas
before, during and after this great adventure.

Contents

The route map.

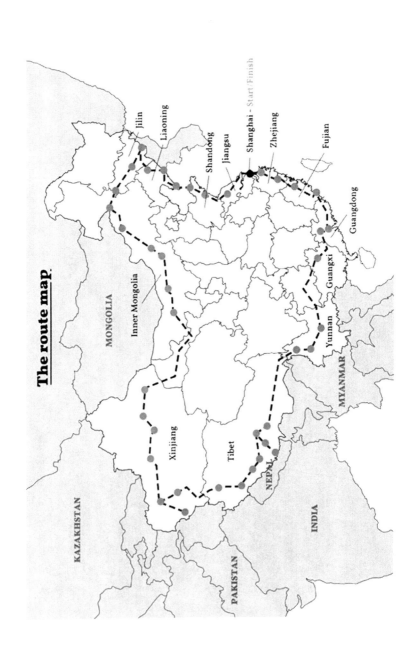

Chapter 1

Crazy decisions and monumental tasks

I'm Ryan. I'm 32-years old, I work as a freelance documentary photographer, and I've lived in China for 8 years.

I've been excited about exploring China since I first came here. For me, part of the pleasure of seeing and experiencing amazing things is sharing them with other people, and photography provides an excellent way of doing that. Since becoming established as a professional photographer, I'd enjoyed the degree of autonomy it gave me and the fact that I was able to find my own stories and work on projects that really interested me, funded by the newspapers and magazines that regularly publish my work. Things were going great.

Then, in September 2008, Lehman Brothers fell spectacularly apart. The cracks that spread almost overnight throughout the corporate and banking worlds soon began to appear in other areas of business too – including the publishing industry in the US, which comprises a large proportion of my client base – and things began to change.

Even before 2008, US publishers were slipping into freefall. The trend for online advertising – especially for classified ads – had already wreaked havoc and had left gaping holes in the balance sheets of some large, reputable, publishing companies. Subsequently, when interbank lending was frozen, companies that had been spending hundreds of thousands of US dollars on annual reports and advertising campaigns stopped doing so.

I had close friends in the US – some really talented people – who lost their jobs: one minute they were on top of the world and the next they were worrying about how they were going to pay huge mortgages on homes that were no longer worth what they owed on them. I knew that my own situation in China was pretty good compared to what they were facing. But I'd recently lost some major clients who could no longer afford my services or who'd 'permanently postponed' jobs I'd thought were done deals, and I was becoming increasingly nervous. It was the first financial slowdown I'd ever experienced, and it made me realize just how exposed and vulnerable to outside influences I really was.

If you're self-employed, as I am, you have control over your own destiny when the economy is doing okay, everyone's spending money, and there's plenty of work on offer. It's a different thing altogether in a recession, however, and the sense I'd had that I was riding the crest of a wave had recently given way to nagging anxiety.

While other countries struggle to pull themselves out of financial crisis, China is booming, and Shanghai, where

I live with my wife and two children, is rapidly becoming an international hub for business and culture. Being on the spot as China goes through an era of accelerated change and development is exciting, on both a personal and a professional level. But although I work largely within China, almost all my clients are in the US, Canada, and the UK, and therefore my ability to find funding for the projects I want to do is governed by the recession taking place in those countries.

When I arrived in New York in March 2010 for my annual round of meetings with editors at the offices of the magazines and newspapers that publish my photographs, I didn't know if they had any money at all to spend on new projects. What I *did* know was that to stand a chance of reversing the slow trickle of canceled jobs that had halved my income in the last fiscal year, I had to come up with some ideas that were sufficiently ambitious and exciting to persuade the editors to fund them from their much depleted and still dwindling resources.

Most of the people with whom I'd managed to fix up meetings were doing their own work as well as that of two or even three other employees who'd lost their jobs. They all had basically the same message for me: 'We love your work and we hope we can do something with you in the future. Right now though, things are still a bit crazy.' It was clear that the economic gloom hadn't lifted.

Every time I left another office, I felt slightly more dejected and slightly less confident. I began to wonder if perhaps my career had already peaked and I was about to start sliding down the more slippery side of the slope I'd been climbing for the last few years. I suppose in my heart I knew that wasn't really true – I do sometimes have a tendency toward the over-dramatic. But it's how I felt as I walked through the afternoon sunshine to meet my brother, Colin, for lunch in Central Park.

Colin had flown down to see me from Toronto, where he was working as a currency trader. At the age of 29, he'd already set up his own company, which had become very successful, and when it was bought by another, larger, company, he'd made a substantial amount of money out of the sale. Part of the deal had been that he would work for the large company for a couple of years. The only problem was that Colin is creative and likes to move as fast as he thinks, whereas the cogs in big corporations, like the one he was now working in, grind slowly and ponderously. The change of pace was driving him mad, and he'd jumped at the chance to take a break for a couple of days and meet me in New York.

There was more warmth in the sun that afternoon than was normal for the time of year, and when we'd bought some Subway sandwiches and a couple of cans of Snapple lemonade, we sat on the rocks above a children's playground at the southern end of the park. I told Colin what had happened at my meetings and we were exchanging stories about the effects the recession was having on the lives of people we knew when he sighed and said, 'I feel as if I'm on a treadmill. It doesn't matter how fast I run, I'm not going anywhere. Somehow, my life seems to have lost its meaning.'

Unlike me, Colin tends toward understatement rather than dramatization, and I felt bad for a moment because I thought my own gloom and despondency had brought him down. Then I realized that what he was saying was something he'd been thinking about for some time.

'My friends and all the people I work with are doing exactly what I'm doing,' he said. 'We live in big houses, earn huge salaries, and have all chosen the same path. Money – the pursuit of it, the spending of it, and the worrying about it – will become the focus of everything I do. I'm living what most people would consider to be the great American dream, and although it seems ungrateful to say so, it isn't what I want. I need to do something that will change my life.'

'It's the first time I've ever heard you talk like that,' I told him. 'I'm sorry you're feeling dissatisfied, but I have to admit that I'm glad you're thinking about following a different route.'

'I'm going to resign from my job.' The words burst out of Colin as if they were escaping. I didn't want to jump in and say the wrong thing, so for a moment I just looked at him, and then he added, calmly and decisively, 'I've worked the two years I contracted to do, and now I'm going to have a gap year. We'll sell the house, put everything in storage, and then Emma and I will go traveling.'

I'd always known that my little brother was capable of making bold decisions, but, even so, I was taken aback by the certainty I could hear in his voice. He didn't joke or speak in a tentative way, as if looking for approval, and I could tell immediately that he was perfectly serious. What I wanted to do right then was whoop with fraternal pride. But it was Colin's moment, so I just nodded and told him again that I was glad he'd come to that conclusion.

I thought I knew how he must be feeling. I'd spent a summer working 16 hours a day for a large company and then 'relaxing' with colleagues every night by drinking excessive quantities of booze. I'd been making a ton of cash – which, for an otherwise impoverished student of International Politics at the University of Toronto, was a very big deal. However, as my bank balance increased, my soul seemed to diminish, and it was partly because of that experience that I moved to China after I graduated, at the age of 23.

In many ways, going to live in China had been a leap into the dark. Now, more than 8 years later, I loved my work traveling around the country taking photographs and I felt that I'd molded my life into the shape *I* wanted it to be. For the last few years, while Colin had been working hard at his desk in Toronto, I'd been getting paid for climbing mountains in Tibet and for exploring some of the remotest and most spectacular parts of China. So my reasons for wanting to shake things up and *do* something were different from my brother's. Having built up some good contacts, I'd let things slide a bit and had become reliant on those people always being there so that the money would keep rolling in. And then I'd realized that if I didn't find some other way of funding my creative pursuits, I was going to risk losing control of my working life.

Colin hadn't been jealous of the way I'd been living – he'd made a very good life for himself – but he'd always been interested and intrigued when I told him about what I was doing and seeing. The main thing that had stopped him traveling with me before was the fact that he was always working. Now, though, if he was going to give up his job, perhaps I'd have an opportunity to share some of my experiences with him.

'Maybe you could start your travels in China,' I suggested. 'We could do a trip together, re-connect with each other.' I punched his shoulder excitedly. 'That's it! That's what we'll do! Where shall we go? I know! We'll go to the Muslim area, Xinjiang, or maybe Tibet, or the holy mountains in central China.'

Colin was instantly as enthusiastic as I was and suddenly my head was buzzing with ideas for the great adventure we were going to share. Wherever we went and however long we were away, it would be the longest quality time we'd spent together since we were kids. It felt as if the blind alleyway I'd been trapped in had opened out into an eight-lane highway, and my spirits, which just a few minutes earlier had been so low, were soaring.

We sat on the rocks in Central Park, joking and tossing ideas backwards and forwards between us. Then Colin asked the deceptively simple-sounding question that set in motion a chain of events with the potential to change our lives: 'How easy is it to ride a motorcycle in China?'

I could feel my heart start to thump the way it does when I know something has just happened that's going to turn a good idea into pure gold.

Colin and I are both avid motorcyclists, although previously only city riders – Colin rides a BMW R1200R he bought a few years ago, and I've got a recently imported BMW F800GS – and as soon as the idea was out there, it became the *only* option for our trip.

'That's it!' I shouted again. 'We'll do a motorcycle tour to some remote part of the country. We need a map.'

It was only as we slid down off the rocks that we became aware that the children had gone, the playground below us was deserted, and the sun had dipped behind the trees, taking with it all the warmth of the day.

At the Apple Store on Fifth Avenue and Central Park South, we went downstairs and brought up Google Maps on one of their iMacs.

'From Shanghai, it's about 1300 kilometers north to Beijing,' I said, 'and about 2000 kilometers west to Chengdu, the capital of Sichuan Province. It all depends on which way we want to go.'

As the older brother and the one who knows China, I wanted to choose a route that would ensure Colin saw the most interesting parts of the country. The problem was that the possibilities were almost endless. Then a thought struck me. Snatching the mouse out of Colin's hand and pulling the keyboard toward me, I began to enter into the computer various locations that would enable us to make a counter-clockwise circumnavigation of the whole of China.

Colin gave a bark of laughter as the route appeared on the screen – north from Shanghai to the border with North Korea, then west to the border of Pakistan, down to Tibet, to Hong Kong in the south, and finally up the east coast back to Shanghai.

'How far is it?' he asked, bending down to get a clearer view of the 'total distance' figure displayed in the corner of the screen.

'Twenty thousand kilometers,' I told him, and when I turned to look at him, we both grinned like over-excited kids.

It was an audacious route; we didn't even know if it was possible to travel it, for practical and logistical reasons as well as in terms of the potential risks involved. And, quite apart from the route itself, there were our wives' reactions to take into account when we told them, 'Honey, we think it would be cool to travel 20,000 kilometers around China on motorbikes. That would be okay with you, right?'

It was at that point that Colin and I decided we needed to think things through before we told Jasmine and Emma anything at all, so that we could make a really good argument in support of what we wanted to do.

Whatever the pitfalls might be, we were both aware that right there on the computer screen, staring us in the face as we stood in the Apple Store in New York, was a *real* adventure. We already knew we were going to do it; it was just a case of working out how.

'We should document it,' I told Colin. 'There's no way we're doing a trip as difficult as this is going to be without documenting it. That's my *job*: I'm a *documentary* photographer. I don't go anywhere or do anything I think is cool or interesting without taking pictures. I'll find a cameraman and we'll make a film.'

'Who's going to want to watch it?' Colin raised his eyebrows and his tone was skeptical.

It was a reasonable question. Although I know about taking photographs, writing articles, and selling them to newspapers and magazines, I knew absolutely nothing about making and editing films, let alone finding broadcasters prepared to air them on TV. But I was certain *someone* would be interested.

'Perhaps we can get National Geographic involved,' I answered. 'Or the Discovery Channel. And we could do a book. I'll work out some costs. Let's make this happen, Colin.'

I was so energized I could almost feel the adrenalin pumping through my body. The prospect of sharing a journey with my brother was really important to me, and if it *did* turn out that there was some way we could enable other people to share it too, that would be even better.

Committing to the adventure that had become a reality in just a couple of hours during that afternoon in New York was a big step for me; but it was nothing compared to the step Colin was taking. As soon as he got back to Toronto, he talked to his wife, Emma, handed in his resignation at work, and put their house on the market.

Despite the fact that funding the trip would involve a significant financial commitment for both of us, it wasn't enough to break the bank, so the money itself wasn't a really big deal in those terms, and spending it didn't require a huge family decision. The only real issues were related to the length of time we were going to be away – which we estimated would be around 60 days.

Colin's wife supported his decision to take a gap year from work and, surprisingly, neither she nor my wife, Jasmine, put up any real resistance to the idea of the trip we were planning to do together – which, it turned out, was because they didn't really believe it was ever going to become a reality. I guess that's why Jasmine was able to smile as she told me, 'You want to circumnavigate China on motorcycles? That's fine. Go ahead. Oh, you want to leave in 6 months and you'll be away for 60 days, while I stay here, alone, with the children? No problem.'

If anything, their lack of belief only served to increase our fighting spirit!

While Colin was putting the first 29 years of his life into storage in Canada, I was in Shanghai, infused by a sense of energy and purpose and doing some serious research. There was a multitude of problems to solve, practical issues to deal with, and lists of questions that seemed to grow longer every time I found an answer to one of them.

What's the best motorcycle to ride round China? What equipment do you need on a journey that will take you on some of the busiest as well as some of the remotest, least traveled roads in the world, through snow-capped mountains and parched deserts? How do you find sponsors for a trip like that? How do you find a broadcaster that might be willing to commit to a film not yet made about a motorcycle journey undertaken by two Canadian brothers no one has ever heard of? Ditto a publisher for a potential book? Was there some way we could use what we were planning to do to raise funds for a charity?

When I'd first arrived in China in 2001, I'd traveled round the country via a route similar to the one we were planning, on buses and trains, and on foot in areas where there was no public transport. That journey had changed my life – not least because it had made me realize that China was where I wanted to live – and there were very few things that could have deflected me from my goal once Colin and I had decided to travel together. So it was probably just as well I didn't know beforehand how complicated and time consuming it was going to be to plan a circumnavigation of the entire country on motorcycles.

The target we'd set for ourselves was massively ambitious – some people might say incredibly stupid. There was so much to organize and so many things that could only be done when other problems had been resolved that there were days when I began to doubt if it was really going to be possible to bring the whole thing together at all, let alone in less than 6 months.

But failure wasn't an option. Colin and Emma's house sold as soon as it went on the market; they put almost all their worldly possessions into storage; and Colin worked out his notice at his job while getting all his business affairs in order. So there was no way I could tell him I hadn't managed to organize things at my end and we wouldn't be able to leave in August, as planned.

My wife's life in Shanghai would carry on more or less as normal without me. She invited Emma to stay with her while we were away – so that they could be bitter together! But, after *our* trip, Colin and Emma were planning to take a trip to Australia and South-East Asia, so Emma decided to stay nearer home to make all the necessary preparations.

It turned out that it wasn't just our wives who had doubts about whether we'd actually complete our journey. Almost everyone told us, 'You'll never do it. Your bikes will break down or you'll quit halfway.' It became apparent that it was a view also shared by people at the companies we approached for sponsorship, some of whom said that they might consider coming on board if we found a broadcaster before we left.

The decision to leave in August had been made on the basis of needing to travel in the best weather, and also because it seemed to give us enough time, from the day when the idea was conceived in New York, to get everything in place. 'That sort of trip takes at least 18 months to organize,' was a common response when we told people what we were doing. They were probably right, but as the enormity of the task I'd undertaken hit me and I began to lose my mind, as well as the will to live, on an increasingly regular basis with each day that passed, I consoled myself – a bit – with the thought that I couldn't have sustained the effort of trying to organize everything for any longer than 6 months.

One of the key factors in the whole expedition would be having the right motorcycles for the diversity of terrain we were going to be traveling over, and right from the outset I'd been having talks with BMW in Germany. When National Geographic Asia expressed an interest in the film we were planning to make and I told the guy at BMW the good news, he said, 'We love your trip! As soon as you sign the contract with National Geographic, send us a copy, as well as details of when the show will be aired, and we'll sort out the bikes.'

It was a huge boost – both for its financial potential and for our confidence – but it was short-lived. Having expressed doubts about our being able to obtain permits to travel through Tibet, National Geographic Asia then decided that the production and airing of the show were going to be too expensive. So they backed out, leaving us without a guaranteed broadcaster, which meant that the guys at BMW were no longer able to justify giving us two expensive motorcycles – and *that* meant we were going to have to buy them ourselves.

The motorcycle we'd chosen was the BMW F800GS, which sells for about US$17,500 in the US. However, as we were now going to have to import two from Germany, we'd also have to pay the 100% tax which is charged on 'luxury' goods that aren't made in China.

You might be able imagine the conversation that followed when I told my wife, 'You know I said we would get free bikes from BMW? Well, we're going to have to pay for them. How much? Ah, well, yes ...' I cleared my throat, knowing that it was crucial to sound both confident and nonchalant. 'Including import tax, it'll cost around US$70,000 for the two of them.'

Although Colin's reaction had been rather more measured than Jasmine's when I'd told him the same thing, the pupils in his eyes had definitely dilated as he'd asked, 'And do you think that's okay?'

'I know it's a huge investment,' I said. 'But it's too late to turn back now. We've done too much simply to stop. We can't get bikes for free unless we're going to generate marketing dollars for sponsors. So we'll do this trip and it'll be amazing, and then they'll all be calling us up to tell us they wish they'd sponsored us.'

In fact, the journey had become an unstoppable, rolling process with its own momentum, and abandoning it would have been like admitting we'd been defeated in some way that was far more significant than it might have appeared.

I knew how lucky Colin and I were to have enough money to be able to finance the trip ourselves, and that there are many people who'd love to become involved in adventure motorcycling for whom the costs are a major and insurmountable barrier. Understandably perhaps, my wife didn't share my sense of good fortune.

'We should be spending our money on *us*,' she told me. 'What you're doing is spending it on something for *you*. How is the family going to benefit from this?'

It was a reasonable question, for which I thought – briefly – I had a reasonable answer.

'I know it started out as just an adventure that Colin and I could share,' I said. 'But if we make a film and maybe write a book, I could make a new career out of doing this.'

'If you make a film and write a book and you earn money, you're going to do it again!' Jasmine wailed. 'And that means you'll go away again for two months or even longer, and then maybe again after that. Why would I want to invest in that?'

'Let's cross that bridge when we come to it,' I answered quickly. 'We'll see how this trip turns out before we talk about what happens next.' I had to concede, though – even if only silently, in my head – that I could see her point.

Once we'd bought the motorcycles, I arranged for them to be shipped from Germany to China and then they had to be registered and licensed. We didn't manage to find anyone who was prepared to support us financially, although we did find really good sponsors who backed us by giving us some great equipment, including Oakley, who gave us sunglasses, and a great German company called Touratech, which provided us with all kinds of upgrades for the bikes.

Finding a cameraman proved to be one of the few things that was easier than I'd anticipated. A friend of mine called Chad Ingraham, who's another Canadian living in China and an excellent photographer, agreed to come with us for a fairly minimal fee because he wanted the experience of traveling around the country. When you're going to be living with someone at very close quarters every single day for 2 months, they have to be someone you can work with under any conditions, even when you're stressed and exhausted, both physically and mentally. Luckily, it turned out that Chad was the right personality for the job.

I set up links with SEVA, a charitable foundation that finds solutions for health problems in lower income communities around the world, opened a Facebook page, and created a website. I researched every aspect of our planned route, got most of the permits and documentation we were going to need, found fixers, drivers, and translators to travel with Chad in the support vehicle on different legs of the journey, and checked and double-checked everything I could think of. In fact, during the months of preparation, I didn't stop thinking about the trip even when I was asleep.

And then it was 30th July 2010 and I was in Munich, Germany, picking Colin up at the airport before driving out to the Enduro Training School in Hechlingen. I still couldn't really believe that all the elusive strands – of which there seemed to be an almost infinite number – were coming together and we were just 2 weeks away from setting out on the Middle Kingdom Ride.[1]

I'm someone who only ever does training of any type if it's absolutely necessary. I'm an 'It'll be okay; no problem; I can wing it' sort of guy. But Colin and I both knew that this was one occasion when 'winging it' could have serious, even fatal, consequences. Neither of us had ever done any multi-day motorcycle trips: the longest ride Colin had been on was 2 days on paved roads with a group of bankers in Toronto – which was a day longer than anything I'd done! The 60-day, almost 20,000-km journey that lay ahead of us was going to be intense: around half of our planned route could be considered to be off-road, on surfaces ranging from hard-packed gravel to deep sand, and, if we were unlucky enough to encounter heavy rain, thick, unyielding mud. It turned out that enrolling in what proved to be an incredibly grueling 2-day training course was a good call, and worth every single dime it cost us.

Hechlingen is a small town in the Bavarian countryside, about 100 km north of Munich, where, in the mid-1990s, a former stone quarry was transformed in the Enduro Park, which is now the home of some of the best off-road training available. The courses that are run there are very popular and an absolute must for any serious adventure

---

1   'Middle kingdom' (or 'central country') is the translation of the traditional Chinese word for China, Zhōngguó – so called because when it was first used in the 6th century BC, China considered itself to be the center of civilization.

motorcyclist. Colin and I had chosen to do the beginners'
course, although I wondered if we'd done the right thing
and if it would be sufficiently challenging for us.

I think it was about an hour into the first day's ride when
my already shaken confidence was completely shattered.
By the time we took a lunch break, I'd fallen three times,
lost all the feeling in my left (clutch-hand) wrist, and had a
bruise on my shin between the top of my boot and my knee
pad that was the size of a large grapefruit. The bike had
suffered damage too, in the form of broken clutch and front-
brake levers and a (left-foot) gear-shifter that had somehow
become bent into the shape of a boomerang.

What we did that day wasn't like any motorcycle riding
Colin and I had ever imagined, let alone taken part in. It
covered everything from low-speed maneuvers, to camel
backs, to riding through water, sand, dust, gravel, rocks,
along narrow stone-filled trails, and up and down steep,
dirt-covered inclines.

As I lay on my back in bed that first night, trying not to
move my screaming muscles and joints, I worried that if our
journey around China was even half as tough as what we'd
just experienced, we'd never make it through the first week.
By the time I fell into an exhausted sleep, my self-assurance
was at an all-time low.

The next morning, I could barely lift my leg to swing
it over the seat of the motorcycle. Every vertebra in my
back seemed to be locked into an awkward and unnatural
position, and when I tried to curl the fingers of my left hand

around the clutch, a pain like an electric shock shot up through my forearm and into my elbow. I didn't know how I was going to get through the day.

Then, as we headed up into the hills above the gravel pit on our first group ride of the morning, something miraculous happened. For no immediately obvious reason, my previously jittery, awkward movements became smoother, my stomach stopped churning, and, as if a switch had been flicked, I regained my ability to balance. Suddenly, instead of having constantly to struggle with the motorcycle to try to make it do what *I* wanted to do, it felt as though I was working *with* it. From that moment, I was back in the saddle, and I stopped bitching and started riding.

By lunch break on day two, I was as giddy as an excited schoolgirl, and I couldn't stop grinning. All my aches and pains seemed to have evaporated – or, at least, the fire that had been raging throughout every inch of my body had died down to become merely smoldering embers. For the rest of the day, I was able to enjoy the riding and the world-class instruction we were being given as we learned the skills we were going to need to ride off-road.

The techniques our instructors taught us – for braking and turning and for retaining our balance and body position on different surfaces – were genius, and the sensation of putting them into practice was invigorating. My confidence was soaring and I was having fun. Bring on China!

Colin

6 August 2010, Frankfurt

When you start out in life, you have to make some big decisions, and then, before you know it, you've got a job, a mortgage, and a family; the life you created for yourself seems to have developed its own momentum, and you're being dragged along by it rather than really *living* it.

During the last couple of weeks while Emma and I have been traveling in Europe – to London, Amsterdam, Brussels, Paris, and now Frankfurt – I've had plenty of time to think about what I've just done, quitting my job in Toronto and selling our house and 99% of our possessions. Now, with just 7 days to go before Ryan and I set out on our trip around China, I feel that I want to get started.

I'm nervous about what lies ahead, and particularly about what will happen after this trip. But even when I'm feeling low, as I am today, I know I'd rather have made all the decisions I'm now questioning than one day, when I'm an old man, be full of regret about the things I didn't do.

The real reason I'm feeling down today is because I've just said goodbye to my wife. Although we both knew this day was coming and that it wasn't going to be easy, I'd pushed it to the back of my mind and avoided thinking about it. I had no idea how hard it would really be. Tomorrow, I'll be on a plane to Shanghai without Emma, and I won't see her again for 60 days. I miss her already.

9 August 2010, Shanghai

I arrived in Shanghai yesterday. Coming direct from Germany, which probably has one of the most efficient road systems in the world, one of the first things that struck me about Shanghai was the apparent chaos on the roadways here.

My brother and I spent most of today running around town getting last-minute shopping for our trip. Having lived all my life in Canada, I was astounded by the noise and the lack of space in Shanghai – which, I suppose, are only to be expected in a city with a population of 20 million.

Another thing that's very noticeable about the city is the huge disparity in wealth. It really surprised me. There's probably more affluence here than in many of the world's major cities – certainly more than in Toronto. Most of the really wealthy people are foreigners, Chinese entrepreneurs, and senior business people, who have a great quality of life. In fact, the amount of money you need here to have a good life is far less than anywhere in Europe or North America – not least because labor costs are lower.

Wages for most people are very low and, alongside the incredible prosperity, there's a very marked degree of poverty in Shanghai. Trying to address the issue of inequality is a huge problem for the Chinese government. If it were to raise the minimum wage, some businesses would shut down, and then some people wouldn't have any work at all. So perhaps the rich should pay higher taxes instead. It's a major dilemma, and who knows what the answer is.

Another thing that stands out in Shanghai is the amazing service people give you. They seem to be happy to be living in the city and to have jobs to do, so there's none of the resentment you sometimes sense in some of the people who do similar work in Europe and North America.

Tomorrow, I'm getting my brand new bike, and then all our Touratech gear will be put on it. I can't wait! I'm excited about the trip. There's so much diversity just in Shanghai that I'm really looking forward to seeing the rest of the country.

Chapter 2

Day one: heat stroke and second thoughts

I hated leaving my wife and children; I didn't want to think about how much I'd miss them. Despite all the preparations we'd made, Colin and I were setting out into the unknown, and by the time the day came for us to leave, all I wanted to do was start riding. As soon as we got on the bikes in the early morning of 14 August 2010, the stress that had been building up for the last 6 months seemed to lift like a weight from my shoulders.

The traffic in eastern China is insane. There are literally millions of cars on the roads at any one time, and the frustration generated by the inevitable chaos is at least partly responsible for some crazy driving. As Colin and I rode out of Shanghai, our lungs were instantly filled with the smoke and diesel fumes that spewed out of the trucks crowding the road like the carriages of a colossal, slow-moving, and filthy train.

The temperature was rising steadily and the humidity was high, which is fine when you're riding at speeds of 80 kph or more and the air is rushing in through the vents in your protective gear to keep you cool. It isn't so great at 30-40 kph. At whatever speed you're riding and on whatever road surface, you still have to wear all the gear, because you never know when you might take a fall. So, before long, I felt as if I was slowly boiling to death inside an increasingly damp, uncomfortable, sealed plastic bag, at the same time as being suffocated by hot exhaust fumes and all the crap that was blowing up into our faces off the road.

Despite the volume of traffic that was already on the highway by 6 o'clock on that Saturday morning, it took us little more than an hour to reach the car ferry that would carry us across the Yangtze River. We were physically shattered, and it was a relief to be able to stretch our backs, spit out the thick oily taste of diesel that seemed to fill our mouths, and relax.

The main problem on the other side of the Yangtze was largely related to the fact that most of eastern China is under construction. New roads appear almost overnight and small towns become huge modern cities within what seems to be the space of just a few weeks. One result of all that construction is that the traffic blockages on the roads are unbelievable.

Another problem for us that morning was that the signage on the new roads isn't good. We had GPS on our motorcycles, but you'd have to update it almost daily in China to keep pace with what's going on, and our information was a year old. Almost all the roads had changed: some had disappeared altogether and some minor roads that had previously gone nowhere of any significance had become major highways.

We'd planned to take the G204[2] right up through Jiangsu Province, north of Shanghai – we couldn't even find it. We got caught up in the suburbs and seemed to be going round in circles. At 9 a.m., we stopped in a village to drink some water and take stock. As Colin and I sat on little Chinese stools at the side of the road with our knees up around our ears, it already felt as though we'd lost the plot. We asked a few people how to get to the road we wanted and eventually someone gave us the right directions. We were on our way again, and we could feel our spirits soaring.

The euphoria didn't last long, however, because the traffic on the G204 was wall to wall and we had to creep along at just 25 kph. The way our moods dipped and rose repeatedly that morning, between despondency and elation, pretty much set the pattern for the way we felt throughout the entire trip.

We'd known that we'd be riding on a busy highway that first morning, but we hadn't had any idea what it would be like in reality, particularly in a rapidly increasing temperature and high humidity. It doesn't matter how much planning you do before a trip like the one we were embarking on, it's only when you actually set out that you can really figure out how things are going to work. So far,

---

2   The major, nationwide roads in China are given the letter G – from the Chinese word Guojia, meaning nation; the regional roads are S roads – from the Chinese word Shengji, meaning province-level.

it hadn't been quite how we'd imagined it would be: there certainly wasn't any of the wind-in-your-hair-on-an-open-road feeling we'd anticipated.

Chad, our cameraman, was riding with Ted Hurley, a good friend of mine who'd agreed to be our driver for the first leg of the journey, and Colin and I were trying to stick close to the support vehicle – without the cameraman, there's no film. Sometimes we drove with the SUV behind us and sometimes it went on ahead and stopped, so that Chad could film us coming down the road toward him, which was necessary and planned for, and which slowed us down even more. We also stopped every hour to drink liters of water, in an attempt to replace the fluid we were losing in our sweat, and to shake our legs and stretch the cramped muscles in our backs; and every 2 or 3 hours we filled up the small gas tanks on the motorcycles.

The GPS systems that were strapped to the handlebars of our bikes might not have been very accurate in terms of providing us with up-to-date information about our route, but they *were* reliable as expensively over-engineered thermometers. As we edged our way along the highway, sweating profusely inside our suits and feeling increasingly sick and light-headed, Colin and I talked to each other over the communication system in our helmets.

'It's 39 degrees Celsius,' one of us would say. Then, a few minutes later, 'Now it's 41 … 42.'

By midday, we were exhausted and we decided to pull up at the next place we saw where we could eat, which turned out to be a noodle restaurant.

When Colin took off his helmet, I was shocked by how terrible he looked. He's lived all his life in Canada and although he's always played a lot of sport and is physically fit, riding a motorcycle in oppressive humidity and intense heat was completely beyond anything he'd ever experienced. His face was deathly white and when he groaned and said, 'I feel like I'm going to throw up,' it was clear that he had heat stroke. It was only lunchtime on day 1 of our 60-day journey and I was already wondering how we were going to make it to the end.

Fortunately, the risk of dehydration was something I'd been aware of and concerned about from the outset, and we'd taken with us hundreds of little packets of rehydration salts. We downed a couple of those each, ate some noodles, drank some Sprite and Coca-Cola to replace some of the sugar that had leached out of our bodies in our sweat, and, after about an hour, we began to be able to focus properly again.

At 6 a.m. that morning it had all seemed so exciting, this great adventure we were setting out on. Six hours later, we'd spent an hour on a ferry and 5 hours on the road, and had traveled just 130 km. We'd expected to cover about 450 km that day; it was clear by lunchtime that that wasn't going to happen.

Our slow progress was partly due to the heavy, slow-moving traffic we'd got snarled up in, and partly because we'd got lost a couple of times. We'd been riding on good paved roads – probably the best surfaces we were going to encounter throughout the entire trip – and it was difficult not to start doubting ourselves and wondering if the whole thing had been a huge mistake. Perhaps what we'd set out to do wasn't achievable.

The fact that no one had backed us by giving us money to sponsor the trip meant that if it all took far longer than we'd expected, we'd have to meet the additional costs ourselves – costs that would include paying more to Chad and the different drivers, translators, and fixers we'd hired for each leg of the journey, for more meals for all of us, and for extra nights in hotels. On top of that, there'd be all the technical and organizational issues that would have to be dealt with. I didn't want to think about it all. I'm a failure-is-not-an-option type of guy, so having doubts, however small and conquerable, isn't something that sits well with me.

Colin and I had played competitive sport from the time we started school: we'd both captained basketball teams that had won championships, and I'd continued to play basketball at university. So we share the same never-say-die attitude, which is just as well, because there were moments during that first day when we looked at each other and I knew Colin was thinking what I was thinking: 'What have we let ourselves in for?'

The whole point of filming our experience was that it was like a science experiment, in which we were the guinea-pigs. To our knowledge, no one had ever attempted to do what we were planning to do, which, although exciting, also meant that no one could offer us any advice or a heads-up about what was likely to happen. The pioneering aspect had been part of the appeal before we set out; now, here we were at midday on day 1, exhausted and far short of where we should have been at that time. A bit of certainty about what lay ahead would have been nice.

It's amazing what a plate of noodles, some sugar, and some salt can do for you, and when we got back on our bikes and were on the road again after lunch, we could feel our spirits start to lift. The volume of traffic on the highway seemed to be inversely proportional to the distance from Shanghai, and it wasn't long before we were traveling at speeds of 60-70 kph. Then, at about 4 p.m., we got onto some really good roads – brand new, almost deserted expressways – and were able to hit the throttle and ride at 120 kph. The dirty, stinking diesel trucks had gone, there were few cars on the road, and we were riding through farmland and open countryside in brilliant sunshine, with cool air whistling in through the vents in our suits.

Although I'd planned where we were going to stay each night, we'd agreed before we set out that we'd stop at 6 o'clock every evening and sleep wherever we were: motorcycles have only one small headlight, which illuminates a very limited area of the road ahead of you, and it's dangerous to ride them in the dark. In China, however, not being able to see in the dark is less of an issue than not *being seen*. People don't use the mirrors on or in their cars, so they don't even notice you coming up behind them on a motorcycle; and if a driver wants to drive on the wrong side of the road for some reason that might seem inexplicable to the casual observer, then that's what he does, even on a highway. Some of the driving is horrific.

We'd been making good time that afternoon and by 5.30 we were just 100 km away from the town where we planned to stay the night. If we pushed on, we could probably make it.

As we stood at the side of the road for what we hoped would be our last stop to drink water before reaching our destination, a white flash of electricity suddenly lit up the sky, followed a couple of seconds later by a loud crack, which sounded like the heavens splitting open. Then it began to rain – just a few fat, lazy drops of water to begin with, which, within seconds, had become a torrent.

It was a relief at first, because the cool air that the rain dragged out of the sky crushed the heavy, suffocating atmosphere that had been intensifying all day and lowered the temperature of our over-heated bodies. The downside was that heavy rain and wet roads are dangerous when you've only got two wheels. So we had to ride at no more than 30 kph, and when I realized that we weren't going to make it to the town after all, I could feel the cheerful optimism draining out of me.

The sky had already been darkened by the storm, and as the sun began to sink out of sight, we pulled off the road at the first place we came to – a middle-of-nowhere town in Jiangsu Province called Funing, which, by a stroke of good luck, had a decent hotel.

Colin and I had agreed that, every night throughout our journey, the first thing we'd do when we checked into a hotel was record video diaries. It didn't matter what had happened during the day – how cold, wet, or close to exhaustion we were – the video diaries were going to come first. That night, we set up the camera in the hotel bedroom and I went outside to give Colin the privacy to speak freely; then he left the room while I recorded my diary; and, finally, we had showers and walked out of the hotel in search of some dinner.

We were both dehydrated, but Colin looked even more wrecked than I did. I couldn't believe how shattered we were after just one day, and I didn't even want to think about the 59 other days that stretched ahead of us. As we were both quite fit, we hadn't done any specific physical preparation for the trip. But motorcycling places enormous demands on the body and uses muscles you don't seem to use for anything else, so it wasn't surprising that, after riding for 12 hours, my body – especially my back – felt as if it had been stretched and pummeled until every single muscle was taut and aching.

We'd done 405 km that day, which wasn't too far short of our target of 450 km. Despite the fact that we'd only managed it because we'd had a couple of good hours after lunch, before it started raining, we went to bed that night feeling pumped.

The worst thing about day 1 was saying goodbye to my wife, which had been an incredibly difficult thing to do.

The best thing about it had been riding with my brother: I'd never done it before and it was an unbelievable experience.

After we'd done the training in Germany, we thought we knew how hard the trip was going to be. We had no idea.

Day 1 *(14 August 2010)*

Day 1 was ridiculous. I didn't think I'd be questioning the trip on the first day; but, man, the morning was unreal. We'd only been riding for about 10 minutes when a cop told us that motorcycles weren't allowed on the road we were on. Ryan darted around the guy, so I followed him. To me that's bizarre, the fact that you can ignore a cop!

A few minutes later, another cop came up behind me, siren blaring, flashing his lights. I was going to stop, and then I heard Ryan's voice in my helmet telling me to keep going. The guy followed me for maybe 5 minutes before turning off, and after that they left us alone. Where else would they give up like that? It's crazy.

It was already hot when we set out. Getting out of Shanghai wasn't too bad, except for the pollution and the trucks – I couldn't believe how many trucks there were on the road so early on a Saturday morning – and we made decent time all the way to the ferry. It was on the other side of the river that the trouble really started.

We drove through countless factory towns and farms. It's amazing how much industry there is in China, although perhaps it isn't so surprising when you think that not only do they have a population of 1.4 billion, they also produce and manufacture all kinds of stuff, which they supply to countries around the world.

We got lost in a little farming village, which had some nice houses and some parts that were remarkably wealthy. It was midday, the temperature was 42° Celsius, Ryan and I were wearing full gear and sweating like crazy, and already by that time I just wanted to get to our destination. Even drinking liters of water didn't make any difference to the way I felt, and when we finally got back on track and stopped for lunch, I was more down than I've been for a long time.

I was very tired and feeling ill, and I wanted to quit; I really thought I couldn't do it anymore. I've never experienced that kind of heat before – I hope never to experience it again – and it turned out that I had heat stroke. Somehow, after lunch, I was able to pull it together and get back on the road, despite still not feeling good. And then, after about half an hour, when the food and the salt and sugar hit me and we got onto a good road, I started to feel a bit better, which was lucky, because if the afternoon had been anything like the morning, I don't know what I'd be telling you right now!

I got a second wind, and it felt like we were accomplishing something. Then it started to rain really hard, which seemed like a disaster, and it was getting dark when we stopped in Funing. I was completely exhausted. It was *such* a hard day; harder than any day I've spent at work, ever.

One of my main impressions at the end of day 1 was that the driving in China is wild. At one point, we were riding on a four-lane highway that had dividing barriers at intervals down the middle. It sounds like a normal road, right? Except that they have crosswalks for small motorcycles, scooters, and pretty much any type of farming vehicle. When you're driving along the highway, you don't stop at these crosswalks: the people who want to cross from one side of the expressway to the other are supposed to pick the right moment. That's great in theory; in practice, however, they go when they want to go. I guess they just hope that you manage to stop before you hit them. It's unbelievably dangerous. And then there are the drivers who decide that they like your side of the road better than theirs, for some reason I haven't managed to work out, so they cross over and drive on the wrong side.

All in all, it was a gut-check day. Luckily, I think I passed.

Chapter 3

North from Shanghai

We woke up at 6.30 on the morning of day 2 feeling great. After a good breakfast, we were on the road by 8 o'clock, which was around the time we aimed to set out every day, especially when it was hot, so that we could make use of the cooler hours of the morning. We continued going north from Shanghai on the G204, which was the same road we'd been on the previous day. The sun was already up when we set off, but the temperature only reached around 30° Celsius, rather than the 40+° it had climbed to the day before, and we were moving fast enough to keep cool.

The terrain we were riding through was almost consistently flat, with farmland on either side of the road in an area that was quite heavily populated. It seemed that every single person who lived for miles around was on the G204 that morning, which meant that the volume of traffic was such that anything that impeded its flow would make it grind instantly to a halt – which was what happened when we'd been riding for about an hour and hit road construction.

Colin and I could have gone round the stationary nose-to-tail line of trucks onto the hard shoulder and kept going, but that would have entailed leaving the support vehicle far behind us, which in turn would have meant that if we'd seen something interesting or something had happened to one of us, Chad wouldn't have been there to record it. So we stayed with the SUV and tried to weave our way through the biggest, most frustrating, most badly managed traffic jam any of us had ever seen.

In places where the road was down to just one lane plus the hard shoulder, the cars and trucks were supposed to be passing each other going in both directions. In fact, nothing was moving except for a few bicycles whose riders were weaving around the traffic and coming perilously close to colliding with the little three-wheeled tractors that were trying to squeeze through gaps the rest of us couldn't even see. There was no sense or logic to what anyone was doing, and every time a truck driver tried to disengage his truck from the jam, it only made things worse – for him as well as for everyone else.

By 9 a.m., our spirits had hit rock bottom. We simply weren't getting anywhere. Colin and I aren't impatient, and we didn't feel that we were in a rush because we *had* to do 500 km a day. But we do both like to feel that we're making progress and going places – even when we're not actually *trying* to make progress and go places, as we were on that day. There were no detours we could take to avoid the traffic jam: we didn't want to leave the road, waste time going into a town, and risk getting lost. So we took deep breaths and tried not to let our frustration overwhelm us.

When we stopped for lunch at a truck stop beside the road and took off our visors, our faces were almost black and our eyes were red and sore – road construction creates an incredible amount of dust. The food we ordered wasn't good and even washing down the contents of some rehydration packs with copious amounts of Coca Cola and Sprite did nothing to alleviate the gloom that had descended on us when we realized we'd traveled just 100 km in 4 hours.

And then, within an hour of setting out again after we'd eaten, we were on a six-lane highway that was almost empty of cars and trucks in both directions, and we were doing 120 kph. We opened the vents in our suits so that the air could flow freely around our bodies and, as we high-speeded it through farmland in the sunshine, we felt as though we were on top of the world.

Despite the way things picked up for us in the afternoon, we didn't make up the time we'd lost that morning and the previous day. We knew we weren't going to reach the town of Qingdao, which is where we'd planned to stay that night, so we decided to stop at Huangdao, which is on the other, southern, side of Jiaozhou Bay.

We were about 50 km from Huangdao, the light was getting low, and the sky had turned an extraordinary pink color I'd never seen before, when the most amazing mountains seemed to rise up in front of us as if from nowhere. It was a breathtakingly beautiful sight and, suddenly, not reaching our intended destination that night didn't matter. We hung out on a beach for a while, watching the changing colors in the sky and just being silly, and then we booked into the Horizon Hotel in Huangdao, feeling pretty good. Later, after we'd done our video diaries and washed off the grime from the road under the shower, Colin and I joined Chad and Ted and we all went out to look for somewhere to eat.

We'd done only 362 km that day. It was the second of the 2 days we'd been on the road when we'd failed to do the distance we'd wanted and expected to cover. I knew before we even discussed it that Colin was thinking what I was thinking. Were we going to be able to complete our journey? Were we going to need 80 or even 90 days rather than the 60 we'd planned and budgeted for? And if it was going to take that much longer, how were we ever going to broach the subject with our wives?

That night, I phoned Jasmine and she asked me, 'How's it going?' I tried to sound enthusiastic as I answered, 'It's going great. Yeah, really great.' But the truth was that, although we'd had a much better day than yesterday and I was excited about what lay ahead for us tomorrow, I was worried. Every day that we were on the road was expensive and the difference between 60 and even 80 days would be significant – not to mention the fact that, physically, the first 2 days had already nearly killed us. Colin still maintains that, for him, the first day, when he was suffering from heat stroke and feeling disorientated, was the hardest of the entire trip – which is surprising, considering the difficulties that lay ahead for us.

In some ways, those first 2 days set the pattern for the remainder of our journey. When we woke up every morning, we never knew whether we were going to do 500 or 150 km; whether the sun would shine and the sky would be a clear, brilliant blue or we'd be riding through torrential rainstorms, so cold that our bodies felt as if they were burning; or where we were going to sleep that night. I'd drawn up a great schedule, which had already become irrelevant and virtually meaningless.

Flying by the seat of our pants was okay during some parts of our journey – when we were in the middle of nowhere in Tibet, for example. In eastern China, where there are towns and villages, road construction and heavy traffic, the not-knowing wears you down. We thought the first few days were going to be the easy ones – after all, eastern China is where 80% of the population of the entire country lives, so it has good, paved roads, hotels, guest houses, and restaurants, and you can buy almost everything you need. It was supposed to be the warm-up to the harder part of our journey that would come next. [Pause for hollow laughter!]

Luckily, Colin and I had each other: even during those first couple of days we were feeding off each other and not allowing ourselves to be negative. Sometimes, when we stopped for lunch, one of us would say, 'We're not going to get to where we need to be tonight,' and the other one would shrug and answer, 'Yeah, but I think it's going to be okay.' We didn't really have to build each other up – we'd got ourselves into this and we were just going to have to roll with it – but when times get tough, it's good to have someone with you to remind you what you set out to do and that, whatever happens, you mustn't lose sight of the fact that you're supposed to be enjoying it.

What sometimes added to the anxiety for me was the sense I had of having a responsibility toward Colin. There were two things that were really important to me: one, that he had a good time, and, two, that he was safe. It wasn't that I thought I had to take care of him: even though I was very aware, as I've always been, that he's my younger brother, I knew he could handle whatever was thrown at us. What he didn't know, as I did, was just how dangerous the roads in China are, so I felt that I needed to stay up front and lead, for most of the way at least. What *neither* of us knew, however, was just how tough the riding was going to be. I can go hiking in Tibet and walk for 12 hours a day for 10 days without complaining, but I didn't know Colin's level of tolerance – I'd never seen it put to the test. As it turned out, I needn't have worried: he was more than equal to all the challenges that were thrown at us.

Even though day 2 was considerably better than day 1 had been, the riding was still exhausting. No distinction is made in China between the small motorcycles that millions of people ride and big, powerful machines like ours – which are almost never seen on any roads in China – and motorcycles aren't allowed on the expressways. So, most of the time, we had to use small, slow, secondary roads, where we averaged about 50 kph and where, because the drivers weren't focusing on what they were doing, we couldn't let our concentration and awareness of the traffic around us slip for even a second. It was that, above anything else, which made those days so tiring.

On the upside, I was proud that we'd got back on track and I was really enjoying spending time with my brother. It was great to be able to have what amounted to 12-hour phone conversations with him through the Bluetooth headsets in our helmets. Sometimes, we'd use them to warn each other about the dangers around us on the road, saying things like, 'Watch this guy: he's coming up fast,' and 'Look out for the tractor on your right.' And when there wasn't much traffic on the road, we just talked – about life and about our plans for the future – in a way we hadn't done for years.

When we left Huangdao and continued up the coast of eastern China, the sky was clear, the air was cool, and there was just enough of a breeze to make it a really great day for riding. Then, on the way out of town, we saw a Starbucks and stopped to have some coffee, which was like a real taste of home.

The road was well maintained, there was no road construction and very little traffic, and we were able to move fast. We were in a remote part of Shandong Province, away from the bigger cities, and by 9 a.m. we were cruising. It was the first morning when we thought we might just manage to get to where we wanted to be at the end of the day.

When you're riding a motorcycle on a journey of adventure, you don't want to go so fast that you don't see anything. On the other hand, it's incredibly satisfying to look down at your odometer at 10.30 in the morning and see that you've already done 150 km: it makes you feel that you're making progress, moving on, getting somewhere.

When I'm traveling in China for work, I'm taking photographs and documenting people's lives, so I stop quite often to talk to people, which is great and I enjoy it. On this occasion, however, the main purpose of the journey I was making with Colin was for us to spend time together and for him to see all the varied and changing faces of the country I'd grown to love. We wanted to have an understanding of what we were seeing, and we hoped we'd have some sort of cultural interaction in the places we stopped each night – which were mainly truck stops, run by families, at the edges of small towns. That interaction would take place when we were *off* the bikes though, which meant that most of the daylight hours every day were all about riding and putting the kilometers behind us.

I've got friends who enjoy simply 'being there' and aren't bothered about *getting* anywhere. Whereas Colin and I aren't drifters by nature: in fact, we're very similar in terms of being goal-oriented. So we settled happily into spending every day seeing things, getting good film footage, and covering ground: it was a really good feeling on the days when that all came together.

Doing a trip by motorcycle is completely different from doing the same trip by car. When you drive a car, you're shut inside a little bubble, there's a physical barrier between you and the world around you, and you're probably using about 2% of your brain. Whereas when you're on a bike, you're *in* your environment, your concentration is 100%, and every one of your senses is alert, all the time. On a motorcycle, you can smell the smells of the city or the countryside you're riding through, you can feel the changes in the direction of the wind and the bumps in the road. You *see* everything around you and above you, and if you want to absorb your surroundings even more, you can just slow down from time to time, pull up your visor, and breathe it all in. In fact, being *in* your environment is one of the main reasons why it's so exhausting to ride a motorcycle, as well as the reason why once you've ridden one, you'll never want to travel by car again.

Colin and I had planned lots of days off when we'd do fun things. But there were other days, particularly during the first week, when we just wanted to push forward and get out of eastern China, where it's crowded, polluted, and not very exciting, and into the really interesting parts of the country – the Mongolian grasslands, the deserts of Xinjiang, the Muslim areas in the north, and the vast remote landscapes of Tibet. So, on the third day, after coffee at Starbucks, it was good to be moving.

After a couple of hours on the road, we stopped for gas. In the West – and in all my previous experiences in eastern China – when you want to fill up the gas tank of a motorcycle, you pop open the cap, stick the nozzle from the pump into the opening of the tank, squeeze the trigger, and the gas flows out. So when we stopped for the first time on day 3 and were told by an agitated, arm-waving gas-station attendant to park off the forecourt, I didn't know what was going on.

Handing us an oversized teapot, complete with handle and spout, the attendant explained that we had to take it to the pump, fill it up with gas, carry it back to our bikes, and then empty its contents into our tanks. Despite it sounding like something dreamed up by a bored TV executive for a reality game show, there *is* a practical reason behind what he was telling us to do. The nozzles on gas pumps in China don't have automatic shut-off, so if you stick one in the small gas tank of a 150-cc bike and it overflows, you end up with gas all over your hot motorcycle engine – which would constitute a fire hazard at the best of time, and particularly in a gas station. It's different with a car, of course, because the gas tank is bigger and the opening to it isn't near the engine. And it's different with an 800-cc motorcycle, which has a 16-liter gas tank. But rules are rules in China, and no amount of arguing, explaining, or reasoning could change the guy's mind: if we wanted gas, we had to use the teapot.

It took at least four fillings and emptyings of the teapot to fill up the tank on each of our bikes, and the whole infuriating, frustrating process consumed 40 minutes. We'd been stopping at gas stations twice a day, which meant that we'd be losing more than an hour of riding time that I hadn't allowed for in my calculations when I'd worked out that we should be able to do 300-400 km that day. I couldn't get my mind round the futility and inefficiency of it all. I didn't have any objection to stopping on the road for something important – like taking a rest, drinking, eating a meal, or visiting someone or something – but I was damned if I was going to spend that much time every day doing something that should take just a few minutes.

Damned or not, it was what happened from that point onwards for many days. Sometimes, I played the part of the dumb foreigner, riding up to the pump and starting to fill up before anyone inside realized what I was doing and came running out to try to grab the nozzle out of my hands. Sometimes, we got away with it; more often, we didn't.

When we got back on the road that day, we were really flying: by the time we stopped for lunch, we'd done 200 km and had our best morning to date. After a good meal, we set off again with our spirits high. The sky was overcast, the sun was only just managing to filter through the thin cloud, and the air was cool. As we rode through tea plantations and gently rolling hills of every shade of green, the world seemed to be bathed in a beautiful reddish-brown light reminiscent of an autumn day in Tuscany. At the top of every hill, we looked down onto the extraordinary vista that was spread out beneath us and I began to relax.

We arrived at Yantai, which was the town we'd hoped to stay in that night, at 4 p.m., 2 hours earlier than we'd expected. It was the first time we'd reached our planned destination and it was a real momentum changer; even Chad and Ted were elated. The weather had been good all day, the bikes were great, and we'd arrived in the coastal town of Yantai in daylight, which meant that, after we'd done our video diaries and had a shower, we still had time to explore the port before drinking a few cold beers and eating our supper in an excellent seafood restaurant beside the ocean.

We were one-twentieth of the way through our journey, on schedule, and, at last, feeling the way we'd hoped we'd feel when we set out from Shanghai 3 days earlier.

Day 2 (15 August 2010)
Today was *so* much better than yesterday, not least because the weather was cooler and we didn't get lost. I *really* enjoyed riding today. We saw some pretty wild things, including some crazy fireworks, which were going off at a store opening. They seem to have fireworks to celebrate anything and everything here.

In the morning, we rode through some bleak, soulless farming and factory towns. It was chaos on the roads, as normal; I'm already starting to get used to people pulling out in front of me or driving the wrong way down the freeway. I think I've figured it out: Chinese people drive with their ears, not with their eyes.

I can understand why it's so difficult to organize and create infrastructure here. China's booming and, as

---

the government transforms the image of what it wants to create into a reality, the sheer size of the construction projects taking place – including road construction and massive condo/home developments – makes it almost impossible to control what's happening.

We had lunch at a small restaurant, where food and drink for the four of us cost 70 RMB – that's around US$10! By the time we stopped to eat, we'd only done 150 km, which was disappointing. Then, at around 3 o'clock, we got onto some amazing roads – although they were just B roads, they had three lanes in each direction – and we were able to make up some time.

When we hit the ocean, I stood looking out across the water thinking how amazing it was to be standing there, with my brother, on one side of China, knowing that, in a few weeks, we'll be on the other side of this vast country.

Tomorrow, we need to do about 350-400 km, which will probably take 6 to 8 hours. Then we'll stay in a hotel for the night before catching the ferry for an 8-hour crossing the next day.

I'm feeling much better than I did yesterday. All in all, it was a good day.

Day 3 *(16 August 2010)*

Last night we stayed in a really nice hotel and this morning Ted and I had awesome Thai massages. The masseuse walked all over my back and worked out some of the kinks. Then we found a Starbucks. I drink a lot of coffee, so it was good to be able to fuel my habit and get some real caffeine into my body.

When they wouldn't let us use the pump at the gas station, my brother had to run backwards and forwards with a tiny teapot to fill up our bikes, as if he was playing some stupid high-school game. It was my first real experience of the Chinese culture of rules.

Some people seem to be totally unable to accept that while they need to apply the rules most of the time, there are some situations in which it simply isn't logical to insist on doing so. Is it a management thing? I'm not sure. What I *do* know is that you need to empower people to make decisions that are appropriate to unique situations, rather than making them follow blanket instructions blindly and never think for themselves. But maybe that's the point.

They gave us a lot of attitude at the gas station this morning. Although I couldn't understand what they were saying, I could see clearly that they were very annoyed with us. It's something you don't seem to encounter in smaller towns, just in the bigger ones.

When we'd filled up with gas and hit the road, we had the best morning yet. The roads were good, the temperature was about 28° Celsius, and it was really fun riding through the countryside with my brother, chatting and catching up on each other's lives, and talking about China. It was wonderful.

On one stretch of the road, we spent about an hour behind a cop car averaging 120 kph, which was great because people stay out of the way of police cars, so it was like being in the car's slipstream on the clear, empty section of road behind it. When we stopped for lunch, we were in good spirits – which were dampened slightly for me by the sight of people eating chicken's feet! It's gross, and something I can't get used to.

Back on the road in the afternoon, the weather was great, the scenery was amazing – I've never seen so many different shades of green – and we had our best 100-km ride so far. It was magical. This evening, we've had a blast in a spectacular coastal town, just relaxing, looking out over the ocean, and eating nice seafood dumplings. It's been a great day.

Chapter 4

A change of plan

After a good night's sleep in Yantai, we rode about 1 km from the hotel to catch the car ferry to Dalian.

Getting onto the ferry was an experience in itself. Despite thinking we knew where we needed to go, we got totally lost. First, we went to the passenger terminal, which was wrong because we had motorcycles, so we weren't passengers. Then, we went to the cargo terminal, which was wrong because we had motorcycles, not cargo. Finally, we ended up at the right place – the automobile terminal.

I'd bought our passenger tickets for the ferry the previous night at the hotel, where I'd been told that we wouldn't need additional tickets for the motorcycles. However, when we arrived at the ferry terminal in the morning, it became apparent that no one has ever been on the ferry from Yantai to Dalian with a motorcycle before. So when they saw our bikes, they stood around staring at them, until eventually coming to the unanimous conclusion that they didn't know what to do.

After they'd all scratched their heads a bit more, someone announced solemnly, 'You have to have motorcycle tickets.' Then, once the *need* for tickets had been established, they all scratched their heads again and addressed the difficult question of how much we should pay for them. Our motorcycles were clearly bigger than Chinese motorcycles – in fact, they were bigger than most of the cars waiting to board the ferry – so should we pay a car fee? Again, no one seemed to know the answer.

In the end, we bought the tickets that the head-scratchers decided we needed and we thought our problems were over – until we were about to get on the boat and the guy checking everyone's tickets demanded to see our 'paperwork'. I didn't know what he meant: what 'paperwork' could he want to see when all we were doing was boarding a boat that would take us from one part of China to another, approximately 150 km across a bay that we could have driven round if we'd had the time to spare?

The man spoke rapidly in Chinese and I couldn't catch a lot of what he was saying, but two things were clear: he was very agitated, and he wasn't going to let us get on the boat, which was due to leave in less than 5 minutes. When I finally figured out that what he wanted were our motorcycle tickets *and* our passenger tickets, we boarded the ferry with our adrenalin pumping and only seconds to spare.

It was a nice boat: our rooms were comfortable and I was impressed by how clean everything was. We did our video diaries, had something to eat and drink, and started to relax. Colin and I would be riding for the next 7 or 8 days without a break, so it was good to be having what amounted to a rest day, and it meant that by the time we'd landed on the other side of the bay, at Dalian, and checked into our hotel, we'd be ahead of the game, with time to prepare for the next few days and plan our route.

The last 3 days had been up and down emotionally. Day 1 had been particularly hard, because although I didn't miss Shanghai much, I really missed my family. On the upside, missing people can help you to appreciate what you've got. I knew, too, that however low the lows, I had to remember how lucky I was to be getting the chance to ride a motorcycle around China with my brother. Despite the weather and the traffic problems, we'd ridden about 1000 km during the first 3 days, and probably had 56 more days to go. If we managed to continue at the same pace and keep safe, it was going to be an unbelievable trip.

We were about to head into Dongbei, the north-eastern part of China, which used to be known in English as Manchuria. It's an area I'd never been to before, and I was looking forward to cruising along the road beside the Yalu River, which forms the border between China and North Korea, and then heading into the remote grasslands and deserts of Inner Mongolia.

Day 5 had its highs and lows too. Chad, our videographer, had been in the process of getting a new visa when we set out from Shanghai and, as it hadn't come through by the time we left, he'd had to leave without his passport, which had now arrived at his home in Shanghai. It isn't legal for foreigners to travel in China without a passport, so it was agreed that Chad would wait in Dalian for it to be sent on to him, Ted would stay with him, and Colin and I would continue on along the coastal road to Dandong, filming ourselves on the way, and then wait for Chad and Ted to catch up with us.

Access to most of the coastal areas of China is restricted and patrolled by the military. But we'd learned from some other riders on a website that there's a great road which runs right beside the ocean between Dalian and Dandong. And they were right: the freshly paved coastal highway that twists its way north from Dalian, with farming villages on one side and the ocean on the other, was stunning and almost empty of traffic.

Around midday, I had a text message from Chad to say that he'd received his passport, everything was great, and they'd meet us on the road. So when Colin and I stopped at a little seafood restaurant for lunch, things were back on track. After we'd eaten, my brother and I cruised along the highway, talking to each other on our Bluetooth headsets about life, the universe, and everything, and feeling as if we were on vacation.

Unfortunately, the theoretical track we were back on had as many twists and turns and switch-backs as the mountain roads, and at about 2 o'clock I got a phone call from Chad to say that the support vehicle had a flat tire, they were getting a push back into Dalian, and they'd catch up with us later.

The best laid plans of mice and men ...! By the time Chad and Ted got back to Dalian and found an SUV dealership, it was too late to source a new tire that day, which meant that they were going to have to stay there for another night and sort things out the next morning.

It was a setback, but not too big a deal, because although Chad and Ted had had a really tough day, everyone was safe and, if everything went according to plan, they'd reconnect with us the next day in Dandong. Colin and I checked into a good hotel and then went out to buy the tools we'd need to do some oil-change work on the bikes the next morning.

When we went to bed that night, the real journey seemed to be just about to begin.

Day 4 *(17 August 2010)*
We had some problems finding the right entrance to the ferry, and then we had to hang around while they decided what to do with us and how much to charge for the bikes. When we got to the boat and Ryan was searching for the passenger tickets, they kept telling us to move out of the way, and he kept saying, 'No. There are only 5 minutes left and if we move out of the way you're going to forget about us and then the ship will leave without us.' So we held our ground, until he found the tickets in his pocket.

We were on the ferry for 7 hours. On the top deck there was a disco-inferno: a whole area where disco music was playing and people were drinking – at 10 o'clock in the morning!

This evening, in Dalian, I went to a Chinese bath house – bath houses are very popular in China, apparently. It was full of kids as well as men and women of all ages, and it was insane! It was the size of a football field, ten stories high, and right in the middle of it there was a stage with performers – in a bath house! It was completely bizarre, like some weird surrealist painting come to life.

Although I'm not really missing Toronto, or work, or a scheduled lifestyle, I *am* missing my wife. But I'm having a blast; I'm enjoying spending time with the guys who are on the trip with us, and I'm really enjoying hanging out with my brother-the-tour-guide.

Everything I'm seeing is brand new to me and every day I see something that surprises me and/or interests me. It's so rare to have an opportunity to experience something new every day for 60 days. And that's what I'm focusing on – on having a good time and getting a feel for China, rather than on the stress of having to get to a particular place every day.

Day 5 *(18 August 2010)*
Day 5 has been a whirlwind. After having to leave Chad and Ted in Dalian to wait for Chad's passport to arrive, Ryan and I ended up on an amazing coastal road, which

isn't on any map, not even Google Maps. We had, hands down, the best day's riding we've had so far.

Chad and Ted are now stuck in Dalian for the night, waiting to source a tire in the morning, and Ryan and I are going to have to slum it in Dandong, without toothbrushes, laptops, or even any proper change of clothes. It really sucks for Chad and Ted, but if they manage to get a tire first thing in the morning, they should be able to join us in Dandong by lunchtime or early afternoon.

We're going to take an unscheduled rest day tomorrow, because we want to spend some time all together in Dandong. It feels a bit like we're sissies, having almost 3 days off in the first 5! I just hope it doesn't carry on the same way, so that we end up circumnavigating China in 180 days!

Despite all the things that went wrong today, it was like every other day so far in that it had a bright side too – on this occasion the fact that my brother and I did 380 km on a beautiful coast road.

Chapter 5

North Korea

There was a viewing deck on the 27th floor of our hotel in Dandong, and after breakfast the next morning, Colin and I went up there and looked out across the Yalu River. Sinŭiju, the town in North Korea we could see on the opposite bank of the river, had no buildings higher than three stories, and even using the high-powered binoculars provided by the hotel, we couldn't see any cars. There were just a few people – all of them wearing the drab, Mao-style jackets and little caps that used to be worn by everyone in China in the 1960s and all of them walking or riding bicycles. You'd expect a town on the border with China to be bustling with all the activities of trade, but at 10 o'clock in the morning it was almost like a ghost town, and there was something very eerie about it.

The main landmarks we could see were the brightly painted gondolas of an old-fashioned, immobile Ferris wheel, and a power plant, which appeared to be functioning, despite signs of some quite significant damage to its buildings, although when we looked across again in the evening, we couldn't see any lights on in the town.

There are two bridges in quite close proximity on the Yalu River in Dandong: the bridge that's now known as the Broken Bridge was built in 1911; and the Friendship Bridge, which was constructed by the Japanese during their occupation of Korea (from 1910 to 1945), was completed in 1943. Both bridges were repeatedly bombed by American aircraft in 1950-51, during the Korean War, in an attempt to stop supplies being transported across the river from China. After the war ended, only the Friendship Bridge was repaired, and it still carries road and rail traffic between the two countries.

There are only four remaining iron spans of the Broken Bridge, which are all on the Chinese side of the river, and about 10 years ago they became a major tourist attraction. The Chinese flock in large numbers to almost anything designated as a tourist site – whatever it is, they book tours to see it and they have a good time – and the Yalu River Scenic Area is highly rated on China's national tourist scale. So, that morning, Colin and I paid our 30 RMB each (about US$4.5) to walk out onto the Broken Bridge with all the other tourists.

Despite everything that's said and written about North Korea, I doubt whether anyone has any real understanding of the country or its people. In his State of the Union Address in 2002, George W. Bush included it with Iran and Iraq in what he dubbed 'the axis of evil' – countries whose governments he accused of supporting terrorism and seeking weapons of mass destruction. North Korea is also called, pejoratively, a hermit kingdom; vast numbers of its people are starving and thousands risk their lives every year when they attempt to escape to China.

Looking out across the water that day, we were maybe 200 meters away from North Korea – so close it almost felt as though we could have reached out and touched it – and I began to get a sense of the paradox that exists in terms of its physical proximity and its disconnection from the rest of the world. Even the fact that we were sharing the experience with a large number of Chinese tourists didn't detract from the surprisingly powerful feelings it evoked.

What we could see of North Korea highlighted the stark contrast between what China was like 30 or 40 years ago and how it is today. Until the 1970s, North Korea and China were on parallel paths, and then, in 1979, China took a different route toward a more open society, embracing capitalist economic reform within a Communist system and creating a great deal of wealth for a small number of people. Modern China may not be a very equal or equitable society, but it does have good transportation and manufacturing infrastructures, which are facilitating its rapid rise to becoming the world's newest superpower. Cars and rooms in good hotels aren't available to everyone in China, but at least they *are* available; whereas North

Korea appears to be shrouded in a cloud of desolation and poverty.

At the time when Colin and I were in Dandong, Kim Jong-Il was still alive and holding the world hostage with the threat of nuclear weapons. His hostile posturing wasn't directed toward China – North Korea depends on China to keep it afloat in every way, and the Chinese seem to feel about the North Koreans the same way we might feel about a slightly crazy, hick cousin. The Chinese government likes to emphasize the Communist bond between the two countries, and the media in China often refer to the people of North Korea as 'our Communist brothers'. In reality, because they aren't allowed to visit North Korea, the only things Chinese people know about it – other than what they can glean from looking through binoculars across the water from Dandong – are that it's cut off from the rest of the world and its inhabitants are poor.

As well as North-Korea-watching that morning, Colin and I also spent some time doing work on our motorcycles. We'd ridden about 1200 km since buying them brand new, so they needed their first oil change, which Colin performed with impressive speed and efficiency. He has an aptitude for doing mechanical and electrical things that I don't have, so I stayed out of his way and documented his skill and dexterity on camera.

Around midday, we talked on the phone again to Chad and Ted, who were still having problems sourcing a tire for the support vehicle and didn't know when they'd manage to sort it out and be able to meet us in Dandong. The day was pretty much up in the air, so Colin and I decided to head for the computer market in town. Most large towns in China have computer markets, and the one in Dandong is massive. We bought some batteries and chargers for our mobiles phones, as well as a few other things we might need if the support vehicle didn't make it that day, and I did a pretty good job of lowering some prices. I think it was Colin's turn to be impressed!

In the afternoon, Colin and I took the bikes out to make sure the new oil was flowing. Riding north out of Dandong along the Yalu River, the mountains were majestic and we could see part of the Great Wall in the distance. At some points, North Korea was less than 100 meters away: it was strange to think how easily we could have swum to it across the water.

Another highlight of the day was playing golf with my brother. We stopped at a driving range beside the river and had a big brouhaha with the security guard because he wouldn't let us park our bikes in the parking lot. The guy insisted that we had to leave them out on the street, and he was totally unmoved when I told him we weren't going to do that because our bikes cost as much as some of the cars in the parking lot and it wouldn't be safe to leave them unattended. He gave in eventually, and Colin and I bought a bucket of golf balls and spent an hour hitting them. With a good driver, Colin can hit a golf ball about 300 meters, and it was very tempting to tee up and see if he could send one over the river into North Korea.

Chad and Ted kept in touch by phone throughout the day and arrived in Dandong in the evening, having managed to source a tire in Dalian. It was great to see them and to have everyone back together again. I'd been worried about them and I'd hated the fact that they were having problems I couldn't do anything to resolve. The trip was my 'pet project' and I wanted to make sure everything went right. Of course, Chad and Ted didn't need me to manage anything on their behalf: they were more than capable of sorting it all out themselves, and they did a great job. Throughout the Middle Kingdom Ride, our support team was amazing, and the help Chad and Ted gave us was invaluable: we couldn't have done the trip without them.

No one likes it when their plans are blown up in the air and an expedition is delayed. But, on that occasion, there was nothing we could do about it: the SUV had a flat tire and the support team took care of everything that needed to be managed. In fact, the unscheduled rest day that was forced on Colin and me turned out to be a special day. It had been a long time since just the two of us had had a chance to spend a whole day together – and spending time with my brother was what the trip was really all about.

When we set off the next morning, we would be leaving behind us the cities and the heavy traffic and heading into the more remote, less-traveled areas of north-eastern China. I was looking forward to it, and I was excited about the prospect of what was to come.

Day 6 (19 August 2010)

I did my first oil change today. Although I knew how to do it in theory, I'd never actually tried it before. It went quite smoothly, and now I'll probably do the oil changes on all my vehicles for the rest of my life.

My brother and I went for a walk to a bridge that used to link China and North Korea. North Korea was just 200 meters away! The current's pretty strong, but you could have swum across the river; in fact, thousands of people do it every year – in the other direction, of course. It was extraordinary to get so close to North Korea and be able to see for ourselves the incredible contrast between the two countries.

What we could see of the town of Sinŭiju looked very poor in comparison to Dandong, although, despite being dilapidated, the houses weren't as bad as some of the houses I've seen in farming villages and industrial towns in parts of China.

I wondered why China cares about North Korea at all; talking to my brother, it seems that if North Korea was thrown into disarray for any reason, the resulting instability could have a bad effect on China – not least because hundreds of thousands, if not millions, of North Korean refugees would try to cross the river. So I guess that's the Chinese government's motivation for doing what it can to help maintain the status quo there.

We also went to a huge computer market today. We didn't know when Chad and Ted would get here, so it seemed like a good idea to have some batteries, phone chargers, and memory sticks – they'll be useful if something similar happens in the future.

Afterwards, we took the bikes for a spin along the river and saw part of the Great Wall, which was really cool. The driving range we stopped at was in a little gated community with a hotel and some condos. The parking lot was full of expensive cars, and we saw a girl with a Louis Vuitton bag and some beautiful Callaway golf clubs – which reminded me again of the huge chasm between the rich and the poor here, and highlighted the even greater contrast between wealthy people in China and the extreme poverty in North Korea.

There are poor people in Western countries who are unemployed and living in slums, but in the UK and the US, for example, there's a minimum wage, so the disparity between the relatively small number of people with extreme wealth and those at the other end of the spectrum who are employed isn't *impossibly* large, which it is in China. Here, there are people driving around in cars that cost US$300,000; some people earn US$50,000 a month and others work long hours every day for maybe US$200 a month. A huge gulf like that isn't bridgeable, particularly in a country where there are so many people – You aren't happy with what you're earning? Well, there are plenty of other people who want your job.

It makes me wonder what will happen in China in the future: it's when the masses realize how far away from the rich they are that revolutions start. Maybe that won't be the case in China: it's a mistake to imagine that the Chinese think like Westerners – they don't. Their culture and the basis of their society are very different from those of any Western nation.

It was really nice to have a day off with my brother today, just hanging out and chatting, which we haven't done since we were in New York the day we came up with the idea for this trip. It's nice to have the team back together, too. Chad and Ted did an amazing job in Dalian and then drove long hours to get here this evening.

I can't wait to get to Tian Chi – the Heavenly Lake. It's supposed to be one of the most beautiful places in the world.

Chapter 6

Flooding in the Yalu River delta

The next morning, we set out to travel along the North Korean border to the Changbaishan National Park. It was going to be a 2-day trip and we had a lot of ground to cover, so it was great to wake up to clear skies.

We stopped off at the Broken Bridge, so that Chad and Ted could look over into North Korea as Colin and I had done the previous day, and then we continued north out of Dandong along the road that runs parallel to the Yalu River. As we wound our way up through the mountains, every corner we turned revealed a view that was even more beautiful than the last one.

We knew it had rained the previous day in the area we were heading into, and we were about an hour into our journey when we met the bad weather. It was some of the heaviest rain I'd ever encountered anywhere and the force of the downpour was unbelievable. Colin and I stopped to put on our wet gear and then we set off again with the support vehicle right behind us, riding at just 30 kph and trying to avoid slipping out on the wet road.

Although the Yalu River at that point is quite narrow, it's fed by a multitude of other, small, rivers and as the deluge continued, we could see a marked change in both the nature and the level of the water. The culverts that have been dug at the sides of the road to drain rainwater off its surface were already overflowing, and the torrent of water that was gushing down the mountainside, sweeping up all the mud and debris in its path, was leaving behind it a dangerous, oily slick.

The riding was exciting but intensely nerve-wracking. Neither Colin nor I had ever ridden in conditions like that before, and I could feel the adrenalin pumping as we maneuvered our bikes through an obstacle course of constantly shifting piles of sludge and rubble that formed on the road for a few seconds before being swept away by the surging water.

The only way to take corners on our bikes was very slowly, which was fortunate, because when we rounded one of them, we came face to face with what at first sight appeared to be the immediate aftermath of some devastating natural disaster. A few cars and trucks had stopped at random angles on the road and alongside it, and at first I couldn't work out what had happened. Then I realized that a huge chunk of the mountain had been dislodged by the cascading water and had come crashing down onto the road, forming a massive mudslide.

Colin and I might have been able to ease our way round the mess on the road, but there was no way the support vehicle could have got through it. There was nothing we could do except sit tight and wait for help to come – however long that might take.

I've often grumbled about the fact that nowhere in China is more than a few kilometers from ongoing road construction. On this occasion, that became a positive, because it also means that wherever you are, you're never far from some sort of road-digging, earth-shifting equipment. While we waited in the pouring rain for a bulldozer to arrive from a nearby construction site, we filmed and chatted to the other drivers and, despite the appalling weather conditions and the uncertain length of the delay that lay ahead of us, our spirits were high.

One of the many surprising things about rural China is the amazing efficiency you encounter in parts of it – sometimes, in the parts where you'd least expect it. It took less than an hour for the guy with the bulldozer to arrive and another hour for him to clear enough of the mudslide for us all to get over or around it – by which time there were some 200 vehicles waiting patiently on both sides. And then we were on the move again, following the road down the slope of the mountain, through several smaller mudslides, until we were back on low ground.

The rain was still torrential and the river was so swollen that it was starting to spill out over the road, which meant that Colin and I constantly had to ease our bikes through deep puddles. Built for off-roading, our motorcycles are quite high off the ground and we were able to ride through water up to about half a meter deep. The main problem in those sorts of conditions is that if one of your wheels starts sliding, it takes the whole bike with it. So the risks were high.

There was one stretch of road, maybe 1 km long, which was as bad as anything that had been thrown at us during the Enduro training course at Hechlingen, and as we stood on our bikes with our knees bent, I could feel the muscles in my thighs burning.

The rain continued to fall and the river level continued to rise until it had become a swirling mass of uncontainable water. At one point, we passed the remains of a bridge that had been washed away, and on many other bridges there were policemen talking urgently into walkie-talkies as they waited for the inevitable moment when they'd have to begin the process of evacuating people from the worst-affected towns. At about 4.30 in the afternoon, we rode through a town called Huanren, near the eastern boundary of Liaoning Province. The rain was still pounding down on us, and we didn't really know how far it was to the next town, but we decided to push on in the hope of reaching it before dark.

Not knowing the distance to the next town was a recurring theme throughout our journey. In China, you can't put the address of a hotel into a sat nav and say, 'That's where we're going to end up tonight,' because addresses, as well as the directions and roads shown on the sat nav, are often wrong. A sat nav can tell you the name of the town you're passing through and you can zoom in and out of the map to see what's 3 km or 10 km ahead of you. What you can't do with any confidence, however, is set a course to follow, because there's a good chance that the roads have changed.

We'd only gone about another 5 km by the time we realized that carrying on in such terrible conditions was a bad decision. So we turned round and went back to Huanren, where we stayed at a bleak hotel called, in English translation, the Rocking International Hotel. Colin and I each had just one pair of boots, one pair of leather gloves, one jacket, and no wet-weather gear: I guess we hadn't envisaged how bad the weather might be. We'd just ridden for 10 hours through relentless rain and now we had to try to find somewhere within the cramped confines of our hotel rooms to hang up the sodden clothes we were going to have to wear again the next day. It's a demoralizing thing, putting on soaking-wet clothes in the morning.

After riding from dawn to dusk in appalling conditions, we'd covered only 230 km, which was a far shorter distance than we'd planned to do that day, and in the evening we talked about what might lie ahead. We particularly wanted to continue to travel along the border with North Korea, because it was a route that took us as far east as it's possible to go in China; but we were worried that the flooding might force us to change our plans, or, at the very least, that we might get stuck somewhere for what could end up being several days.

We'd seen villagers watching the rising water with obvious anxiety and we knew that if people who'd lived all their lives beside the river were anxious, the flooding was a really big deal. It wasn't until later, however, that we read in Reuters about the evacuation by the Chinese military of 100,000 people from the area we were riding through.

It had been a hard day, as well as an exhilarating one, and it had highlighted something that was really important to me – the fact that my brother and I were able to communicate really well. We'd talked to each other constantly throughout the day, including about what level of risk was acceptable to us, the risks we were taking, and whether or not we wanted to continue to take those risks, and we'd agreed on every issue.

It was day 7 and China had already thrown us some curved balls: we'd ridden through intense, suffocating heat; the support team had had to deal with a flat tire; and we'd had two days of hammering rain, landslides, and swollen rivers. We were being tested both physically and mentally, which is pretty much what we'd expected, and I knew that good communication would be vital if we were going to be able to deal effectively with the challenges that lay ahead for us. So it was good to know that Colin and I felt the same way about what was possible and what wasn't.

When we woke up on day 8, we had a hot breakfast, put on our still-wet clothes and left Huanren at 8 a.m. to ride through the rain again. We did 12 straight hours that day and covered about 350 km, in incessant rain, on flooded roads beside rivers whose banks were barely perceptible, and through several landslides, which, fortunately, were just small enough for us to be able to ride over and around them.

It's demoralizing and exhausting when the rain never lets up. You're cold, you have to drive slowly, which means it takes far longer to travel a specific distance than it would in better weather, and as water pours off the mountains, it washes away the small rocks from the surface of the road, leaving debris and mud in its wake. We passed several rivers that day that had breached their banks and flooded the roads beside them, and we were often riding through water that was knee deep. And then there's the pure, wearying, demoralizing discomfort of it all: when you're sitting on a motorcycle, your legs are over the sides, so when the rain comes down, it builds up around your crotch, soaking through your clothes and making your bits wet and cold.

We'd almost reached the town of Baishan, in Jilin Province, by the time the road conditions began to improve. Although it hadn't stopped raining, the terrain had become less mountainous, the road was straighter, and most of the water that continuously pummeled its surface was being filtered off so that we were no longer riding through standing water, which is what's really dangerous when you're on a motorcycle.

At Baishan, we stopped to drink some water and try to relax the stiffness in our shoulders for a few minutes. We'd made much better progress over the last few kilometers than we'd made earlier in the morning. Even though it was still raining, at least we now had traction: we could actually feel the road through our tires and when we hit the brakes, our bikes stopped. A little while later, we turned off the main road onto a smaller, secondary road that would take us to the Changbaishan National Park.

You won't, I'm sure, be surprised when I say that there was a lot of road construction taking place in the national park! While many other countries had been struggling through economic downturn and recession, the Chinese government had recently provided the country with an US$800 *billion* stimulus package, and a lot of that money went into improving the transport infrastructure. Even projects that wouldn't normally have been considered necessary were approved – all you had to do was apply for funding to expand a road and you were more or less guaranteed to get it.

As a result of China's newly expanding affluence, car sales increased by 35% in the year 2010 and, for all the main car manufacturers, China is now the largest market in the world, which is another reason why all the existing roads are being improved and extended and new roads are being built. The road construction in the Changbaishan National Park isn't for individual car owners, however; it's mainly for the tour buses that are used by newly prosperous Chinese tourists who now have the money to visit the burgeoning tourist sites.

The work that's taking place on China's roads will be a good thing for the country. On a purely personal level though, it made parts of our trip extremely tough, particularly when it rained – when you dig up roads in the rain, you create mud, which soon covers every surface with an oily slick that's potentially lethal to anyone riding a motorcycle.

We were just 10 km from the hotel we were going to stay at that night when the accident happened. I always tried to ride ahead of Colin, so that I could set the pace, and I'd been ahead of him for the entire day. I guess he thought I was going too slowly and he got frustrated, and after we'd stopped to drink some water, he zipped ahead of me.

He was probably riding at a fairly reasonable speed, but, in my role as big brother, I thought he was going a bit too fast. Colin's more reckless than I am – I don't know if he'd agree with that statement. I'd say that he's a risk-taker, whereas I'm more conservative. It's all relative, I know, and some people might be of the opinion that the fact that it had been *my* idea to ride motorcycles around China in the first place rather negates any claim I might make to being a conservative man!

Colin does like to move faster; not because he's impatient, he just enjoys pushing the limits more than I do. Or maybe my sense of caution is simply due to the fact that I know China, and I know that even if the road you're traveling on is great, around the next corner there might be no road at all.

Colin had just rounded a corner ahead of me when he hit some loose gravel and then a patch of mud. When I reached the same spot a few seconds later, it was like trying to ride on an ice rink. I only just managed to keep my bike upright, but Colin lost control of his and he went down. You can't use your brakes when you're riding a motorcycle in conditions like that. So I put both my feet down and slid with my bike through the mud. I did use my brakes when I'd stopped sliding, and then I turned the bike around and went back to where Colin was lying on the ground.

'It's okay,' Colin called, lifting a gloved hand above his head. 'It's okay. I'm fine.'

The support vehicle had stopped a few meters further up the road and as Chad ran back toward us through the rain with the camera, Colin raised his visor and then eased his helmet off his head.

We'd been through lots of mud, which, until then, had all been on dirt and rocks that you can push through if you stand up on your bike's foot pegs. This was different, however: although the layer of mud wasn't deep, the surface underneath it was tarmac. Whoever hit that slick first was going down, and when Colin's back tire slewed out sideways, he fell backwards off his bike. If you're going to fall, backwards is a safer way to go than over the handlebars, and when Colin's body hit the ground and he slid about 10 meters, the mud protected him from coming into direct contact with the road surface, which would have ripped open his jacket so that he'd have been badly cut.

His bike slid too, at least another 10 meters, and when we went back to pick it up, there was so much mud on the road we could barely stand upright and lift it. When a bike hits a concrete road, it stops or it flips, and it gets scraped and scuffed, or worse. When it hits mud, it can escape without a scratch, as Colin's bike did. Luckily, there was also barely a scratch on Colin.

You can't embark on a 60-day motorcycle journey around China and think you're not going to fall. Psychologically, however, that was a very bad moment for me and my first real scare of the trip. My little brother had taken a wipe-out and I was surprised by how shocked I felt about what had happened. It was the first time I'd had a sense of, 'Hang on: we don't want to put ourselves at physical risk so that one of us ends up in a wheelchair.' For me, Colin's accident was a wake-up call. It was day 8, we'd had our first potentially serious fall, and Colin had been really lucky. It was time to bring safety up a notch and slow down, even if that meant not getting to where we wanted to be every night. I think it was a wake-up call for Colin too, because after that day he was more careful.

When he got back on the bike, he was still covered in mud from head to toe, and after we'd checked in to our hotel in Changbaishan, he walked into our room and straight under the shower, wearing all his gear. Hosing him down clogged up the drains, the unclogging of which resulted in an extra US$20 being added to our bill the next morning!

When we were riding through a small town earlier that day, I'd seen a man with hunched shoulders and a tired, resigned expression on his face trying to sweep water out of his house. It was clear that the rain was seriously affecting people's lives, as well as destroying their crops, and I knew there'd certainly be some flood-related deaths – even little streams had become raging torrents that were moving fast enough to knock over an adult or wash away a child. That night, I read on the internet news about rivers that had burst their banks and about the evacuations that were taking place in the area.

I'd been worried because the rain and flooding were affecting us on a personal level: the last 3 days had been exhausting for Chad and Ted, as well as for Colin and me, and I'd begun to dread having to put on the same wet boots and clothes every morning – riding a motorcycle when you're cold, wet, and uncomfortable eventually takes its toll mentally as well as physically, by blunting your senses and making you less alert. I was also concerned about what we'd do if it didn't stop raining and we got stuck where we were for days. But what the news reports made me realize was that we were riding our motorcycles through what had become a natural disaster zone, and our concerns were petty compared to those of the Chinese people living in the region, who *really* needed some respite from the rain and some time to recover and repair their homes and businesses.

Day 7 (20 August 2010)

Today was the first day that felt like a real adventure.

As we were leaving Dandong, we went back to the bridge Ryan and I visited yesterday, and Chad got some good footage. Then we rode along the North Korean border, through rolling hills in good weather and I felt real joy.

Rule number one when it comes to the weather in China is that there *are* no rules except for one, which states that whatever is happening at any particular moment won't continue to happen for very long. So, when it started to look like rain ahead, we decided to barrel through and not stop for lunch. We *did* stop to put on some more clothes when the torrential downpour began, but even the heavy rain didn't dampen the good vibe: there's something about an adventure and a challenge that gets the pulse racing, and I was pumped. I loved riding in the rain.

Then we hit a landslide: a section of the mountain had collapsed and been washed across the road, blocking it completely; it looked as if the whole road was moving slowly down the hill. The mud was more than half a meter thick and like quicksand, so even if we'd been able to get through on the bikes, the SUV would have sunk into it.

You hear stories about how long it can take for anyone to do anything in China, and as this was *rural* China, I thought we were going to be stuck there for days, until the rain stopped, the mud dried out, and we could ride over it. So I was amazed when a bulldozer appeared and we were on our way less than 2 hours after we'd stopped. The way they got things moving again so quickly was a real tribute to Chinese efficiency.

When the rain kept falling, we began to realize just how much destruction it was causing. The roads were strewn with debris, rubble, and mud, and the river was flowing so fast you could almost feel its power. We rode for about 1 km through a stretch of unfinished road that was completely under water; you couldn't see the stones and rocks that covered the ground, and it was slippery and difficult to ride through. I almost fell at least three times. It was the most enjoyable kilometer of the trip so far!

At about 5.30, we backtracked to a town we'd already passed through, because it wasn't far off sunset and there was no way we were going to be able to navigate roads covered in debris and mudslides in the dark without someone getting hurt or, at the very least, one of our vehicles being damaged. I was soaking wet and starting to get cold, so I was happy to turn round and stay in a hotel in a nice little town with a great view of the river.

I had a lot of fun today and I'm looking forward to seeing what tomorrow brings. Apparently, it's going to rain for at least the next 24 hours, so the chances are that it will be another interesting day.

We're heading for the Heavenly Lake (Tian Chi) in Changbaishan National Park. I've heard a lot about it and I'm really looking forward to seeing it.

Day 8 (21 August 2010)
Today was another crazy day. It was like entering a war zone. There was flooding and debris everywhere and you could see that the landslide we'd encountered the previous day had been repeated a hundred times. The police and military were on every bridge on every river, watching and waiting for the moment when they'd have to call in reinforcements to help with the evacuation process.

Knowing that all those people were going to be faced with the task of cleaning up the mess the water had made of their lives gave me a feeling I've never had before. Living in Canada my entire life, I've been pretty much insulated from that kind of stuff – you don't come across too many natural disasters in Toronto – and I haven't ever seen serious flooding and mudslides. It was pretty upsetting.

I've come on the trip to experience adventure, to step away from day-to-day life and work and to start *living*. It was in that respect that I enjoyed yesterday and why I loved today too.

For the first hour or two this morning, the rain was relatively light, but by midday it was pounding again, so we didn't stop for lunch – drying off some of the water from your clothes and then putting them back on again is worse than them being soaking wet, and it increases your risk of getting sick. The roads got better in the afternoon, and we were clipping along. Everything was going fine: the scenery was spectacular and there were very few cars. It was the first time since I'd arrived in China that I'd felt completely isolated. It's weird that there are such remote areas when you take into account the fact that China has a population of 1.4 *billion*.

As we got closer to the national park, the quality of the roads started to deteriorate again, and when we rounded a corner where there'd been some recent construction work, I hit a patch of mud, spun to the right, and as I tried to correct it by going left, I wiped out.

It was my first fall – *ever*. I'd dropped the bike a bunch of times at the Enduro Park, when I'd only been going 5-10 kph. I dropped it in Toronto once as well, when I was standing still! This time, I was doing about 30 (or maybe it was 50) kph, and it was pretty scary.

All day we'd been riding on either perfectly paved roads or perfectly unpaved roads made of gravel and rock, which is easy to ride on at 30-40 kph. I thought that this road was unpaved, when it was actually tarmac covered in mud, which meant that there was no friction.

The pannier bags really saved me, by preventing my leg from getting caught under the bike, and the mud on the road stopped me breaking any bones when I slid.

The bike chain's a bit loose and my hip's sore, but both bike and rider are fine, particularly compared to how they might have been.

As we get farther away from the big cities, we're becoming quite a spectacle, probably mostly because of the bikes, and because we're foreigners and there aren't many foreigners outside the major towns. Even this morning, when I went down for breakfast in the hotel, everyone was watching me. It's a weird feeling to be the focus of so much attention. In Toronto, and in the West in general, I don't stand out for any reason: I fit in without ever even thinking about it. I like being able to travel unnoticed, which isn't possible in China, and that's something I'm not very comfortable with.

I *cannot* wait to see the lake tomorrow. Afterwards, we're going to head north and, I hope, get away from the bad weather. It isn't just rain; it's an unremitting torrential downpour, and that creates danger that takes some of the fun out of riding. It *is* an adventure, which I *do* enjoy; it would just be nice to have a sunny day tomorrow and to ride on some smooth, clean tarmac. We'll have to wait and see.

Chapter 7

The invisible lake

At last, the day we'd been looking forward to had arrived and we were going to visit Tian Chi, the Heavenly Lake. The lake is at the top of a dormant volcanic mountain called Changbaishan (or Baekdu Mountain), which, in Mandarin, means perpetually white mountain.

The mountain itself is holy to Koreans, and as half of the lake is in China and the other half is in North Korea, the Chinese military were everywhere, controlling the movements of the hundreds of people who were also visiting what is a very highly rated tourist site. We weren't allowed to ride our motorcycles up to the lake itself, or drive there in the support vehicle, because everyone has to go up the mountain in the official tourist buses. And by the time our bus stopped at the parking lot about 1000 meters below the lake, and we'd joined the massive, slow-moving, upwardly mobile procession of people on the steps leading to the lake, it was raining again.

As we climbed up the last few steps, Colin and I talked to the camera Chad was holding, and when we reached the top, we turned to look out over the lake we'd come so far to see – and there, ahead of us, was a shroud of dense, opaque cloud. The rain was almost horizontal, the wind was howling, and the famed Heavenly Lake, together with the magnificent mountains of North Korea that encircle it, was completely invisible.

We'd seen pictures of Tian Chi, so we knew it was absolutely stunningly beautiful, although we'd been assured by everyone who'd actually seen it that no photograph could do justice to the reality – which was why we'd traveled for 3 days, risking life and limb, to get there. And now we could barely see our hands in front of faces.

There was no alternative other than to transform our disappointment into humor, and then to descend the steps we'd just climbed, catch the bus back down the mountain to the hotel where we'd left the car and our bikes, have some lunch, put on all our gear, and set off on the road again.

Changbaishan was the most easterly point of our journey: for the next 6000 km we'd be heading west, which meant at least 20 days of riding into sunsets.

It wasn't raining back at the hotel and, having wasted an entire morning, we were eager to make up some time and see how far we could get before dark. We'd gone less than 30 km when the heavens opened. In fact, it rained so hard that it was like a white-out. Colin and I talked constantly to each other on our Bluetooth headsets. We couldn't see the road ahead of us or each other, although what was even more unnerving was the knowledge that car drivers wouldn't be able to see us either, which meant that we were at considerable risk of being hit from behind. We knew we needed to stop, but we couldn't simply pull in at the side of the road.

We were doing 10 kph, with both feet on the ground, trying to follow a road we could barely see while praying we didn't ride off a cliff, when we came to a gas station. Driving our bikes underneath its overhanging roof for shelter, I called Chad and Ted on the phone. They'd stopped too, and it was an hour before the rain eased off enough to allow us all to get back on the road again. By that time, it was 2.30 in the afternoon, we'd traveled just 27 km, there was a lot of truck traffic on the road, we were soaked to the skin and shivering with cold, and we had no idea where we were going to end up that night. A day that had started badly was growing steadily worse.

By 4 o'clock, the weather and the tall trees that lined the road on either side had contrived to make it almost dark, and Colin and I decided it was time to stop for the day. When the SUV appeared on the road behind us, we flagged it down and I told the guys, 'Pull over at the next town or village we come to. Look for the best hotel – the tallest building – and that's where we're staying.'

We'd wanted to reach Changchun, but we only managed to do 132 km that day and at 4.30 we pulled in to the car park of a decent-looking hotel in a town called Jingyu, in Jilin Province. When Colin and I took off our boots, we poured at least an inch of water out of them, and as we walked toward the reception desk, I could almost feel the warmth of the water I'd be standing under in the shower in just a few minutes' time.

'No foreigners allowed.' The man at the desk raised his hand, palm outwards, as he spoke. 'The town is closed to foreigners.'

'What does that *mean*?' I asked him.

'It means that foreigners are not allowed to stay in this town,' he told me. 'Only Chinese.'

I was usually the one who argued to get us what we wanted when things weren't going our way, but I was exhausted, and as Ted – who speaks flawless Chinese and was our translator as well as our driver – took up the case on our behalf, Colin and I sank onto the floor of the lobby.

A few minutes later, when it had become clear that Ted wasn't getting anywhere and I could feel the last remnants of my energy dripping onto the floor with the rain from my clothes, I suddenly lost it and snapped at the man behind the desk, 'Well, we're not leaving. It's dark, we're freezing cold, and it's pouring with rain. We've been riding for 3 hours in *horrible* conditions. I'm not getting back on my bike and riding another 100 kilometers to the next town. You don't want to be responsible for my death, do you?'

There are lots of military areas and special zones in China that are closed to foreigners, and some that you're allowed to drive through without stopping. On the other hand, I knew that a rule is only unbendable until someone bends it. But, on this occasion, the man behind the desk was resolute.

Whenever a foreigner checks into a hotel in China, they have to show their passport and be registered with the local police, and it was with an air of producing his trump card that the man said, 'The police won't let you stay here. I'm just the hotel manager. I can't do anything to help you.'

Clearly, Ted wasn't giving in either. 'Right, let's call the police then,' he told the hotel manager briskly, and, after protracted arguing and cajoling, the man agreed.

Colin and I were still sitting on the floor, tired, hungry, and shivering with cold, when the man spoke on the phone and then handed the receiver to Ted. A few minutes later, the door onto the street opened and the local police chief walked into the hotel lobby.

'We're not leaving. It's too dangerous,' I told her, hoping that no one had noticed the puddle of rainwater that had formed around me on the floor.

'Well, you can't stay here,' she said, echoing what the manager had already told us a dozen times. 'The town is closed.'

'Why?' The fact that Ted's a big guy reinforced the impact of his sternly confident tone. 'Why is the town closed? What's so special about this town that we can't stay in a hotel here for just one night?'

The police chief wasn't there to answer other people's questions. 'National security,' she snapped at Ted. Then, glancing down at Colin and me, she added, in a voice that was slightly less unsympathetic, 'I can see that you're struggling. But you have to move on.'

When we refused again, there followed another heated discussion, and then the police chief phoned the mayor, who gave us permission to stay – for one night only and on the conditions that we ate at the hotel, didn't talk to anyone, didn't attempt to venture outside, and left, with a police escort, by 8 o'clock the next morning.

All I wanted was to be dry and warm again, and by that time I'd have agreed to almost anything. So we signed all the documents the police chief gave us, I handed my credit card to the hotel manager, and a few minutes later a shower of warm water was driving the numbness out of my body. It was probably 10° Celsius outside. That isn't too bad if you're just walking around, but it's *very* cold if you've been wet all day and riding a motorcycle, when even a cool wind can have a strong chilling effect.

When we were arguing with the police chief in the hotel lobby, she kept telling us, 'It is for your own safety.' We couldn't really understand what she meant and no one seemed able, or perhaps willing, to explain it to us. It was all very mysterious. Just 130 km away from a major tourist destination – the lake we hadn't been able to see – we seemed to have entered some sort of twilight zone. Not wanting to raise suspicions any further by unpacking one of the large cameras from the car, Colin and I recorded our video diaries that night on a small digital SLR camera.

Twenty years ago, virtually all of China was 'closed to foreigners', which is why a lot of people have expressed surprise at the fact that the Middle Kingdom Ride was possible at all. Today, there's a little more access, although there's still a large number of military bases that aren't on maps and whose existence isn't openly discussed. But we had no interest in 'closed towns', except when they could provide us with, quite literally, a haven from the storm.

That night, a policeman slept in the room opposite ours, to make sure we didn't try to sneak out under cover of darkness! They needn't have worried: Colin and I weren't going anywhere. After hot showers, we changed our clothes, ate a shockingly bad dinner in the hotel restaurant, and then fell asleep in our beds, warm, dry, and finally out of the rain.

The fact that we were falling behind in our schedule wasn't a really big deal in itself. It was just that the problems we'd encountered in Jingyu had been a bit soul-destroying, particularly after riding through unbelievably heavy rain every day knowing that we could have been averaging 300-400 km quite comfortably if it had been dry. Two or three days earlier, the temperature had been 27° Celsius; now, it was getting cold, and rain at 10° Celsius is a completely different thing. It was only day 9 and we had a great deal more to do and see. I just hoped we'd have a good day the next day, so that we could get some kilometers behind us.

We did find out later that Jingyu is closed to foreigners because it has been designated a 'special military area', which turned out not to be such a huge secret after all – we read about it on Wikipedia!

Day 9 (22 August 2010)

Today has been a pretty shitty day. I didn't feel great this morning – I'm starting to get really tired – but it was a day I'd been looking forward to because we were going to see the Heavenly Lake.

I was disappointed when it turned out to be like an amusement park. Chinese tourist attractions are very strange and interesting. In fact, I guess they're really no different from those in the West, except it seems that money grabs at every turn here. There were a lot of non-Chinese tourists there too – mostly Spanish and Italian.

We bought our tickets and had a 45-minute bus journey up the mountain. Then we hiked for another 30 minutes up some steps to the top of the volcano, where it was wet and windy, and where we couldn't see anything at all.

On the upside, it was good to get some fresh air and stretch our legs after spending so many hours on the bikes during the last few days. And it was cool to be able to straddle the border with North Korea: there was just a rope, and some guards, who probably thought we were idiots when we kept putting one foot on the other side of it. But not seeing the lake was really disappointing.

Coming down again was ridiculous. We just wanted to jump on a bus and go, but they have all these stops on the way down, which nobody cares about and which turn a 45-minute journey into 2 hours. It was very frustrating. Every time the bus stopped, you had to walk across the road, past all this stuff they want you to buy, and then get back on the exact same bus. It was annoying and a waste of time, particularly when I wanted to get going on the bikes and try to salvage something from what had so far been a dispiriting day.

When we got back to the hotel, it was about half an hour past checkout time and they wanted to charge us for another half a day. Customer service in places outside big cities like Shanghai just doesn't seem to exist. We were big customers – we'd had two rooms and meals for four people – and we didn't want to check out late from *both* rooms: we just wanted to leave our stuff in one of them so that it could continue to dry out while we had our lunch. In the end, we didn't pay anything extra: the woman at reception called the manager and everything was fine. It was exasperating though, and it added unnecessary stress.

The first half an hour after we hit the road was unbelievable: it was 25° Celsius and the sun was breaking through the clouds. I was having a blast and thinking, 'Today could be the day.' It wasn't. It started to rain even harder than it's done before, and within minutes we were soaking wet again. I'm getting pretty fucking sick and tired of riding in a torrential downpour. We're falling behind with our schedule because of the weather, and the frustration is beginning to kill my spirit.

Before long, the temperature had dropped to about 10° Celsius, we were doing 50-60 kph, and we were bone-chillingly wet again. We didn't get on the road until about 2 p.m., and by 4.30 we were exhausted. So we stopped in a small town for the night, which turned out to be 'closed to foreigners'! They've been very nice to us though, and the fact that they don't want us here, potentially checking things out (I'm at a loss to know *what* things!), is fine by me – at least, it is now that they've let us stay. It's just another interesting new experience to add to all the others I'm having every single day.

Now all I want is a good day with some decent weather. Will tomorrow be that day? I don't know. I bloody hope so, that's for sure.

Chapter 8

Summoned by the chief of police

After a good breakfast the next morning, we left the hotel accompanied by a police escort – one car behind us and one ahead of us – which stayed with us until we reached the city limits. And then the day turned out to be a game-changer: we rode 600 *dry* kilometers in about 11 hours and couldn't have asked for anything better.

In just 2 days we'd experienced a complete swing of the pendulum. I'd been so cold and wet when doing my video diary the previous evening that I'd come close to breaking down in tears, and now we were heading north-west in warm sunshine, riding out of the mountains and into grasslands, with wheat fields as far as the eye could see, in a landscape reminiscent of North and South Dakota or the Canadian Prairies.

We drove without stopping through Changchun – which is where we'd planned to stay the previous night – despite the presence there of a Pizza Hut! At one point, keen to make up some of the time we'd lost over the last few days, we jumped on an expressway. Motorcycles aren't allowed on expressways, and because there are almost no bikes bigger than 150 cc in China, there's never been any need to qualify the rule to exclude from the ban larger motorcycles like ours.

When I stopped at the toll booth at the entrance to the road and asked for a ticket for a car, the toll-booth operator refused to sell me one – in fact, he refused to sell me a ticket of any kind. So I kicked the bike into gear and maneuvered it around the barrier and onto the road, followed a few seconds later by Colin. We'd done the same thing before and got away with it, but this time we'd only gone about 20 km when we came to a road block, which, it soon became clear, had been set up specifically for the purpose of stopping *us*. It was the first time I'd ever seen anything like that in China.

The security guards who pulled us over were clearly annoyed. 'Not allowed,' one of them told us angrily. 'No motorcycles on the expressway.'

'I didn't see a sign at the toll booth,' I answered. 'I'm not aware of any law that says that.'

But the security guard was adamant. 'Follow us to the next exit,' he demanded. 'And then get off the road.'

I tried to explain my point of view: that although the rule was sensible when applied to motorcycles with small engines, which can't go fast enough to keep up with the rest of the traffic on the expressway, 800-cc motorcycles can cruise along at high speeds quite safely. The men weren't interested, so Colin and I had no choice other than to follow their car as it pulled out into the traffic.

The speed limit on the expressways in China is 120 kph, but, for some reason, the guy was doing only 40 kph, which meant that we were being overtaken by huge speeding trucks whose drivers didn't notice us until it was almost too late and they had to pull out abruptly to avoid hitting us.

'This is too dangerous,' I told Colin over our helmet sets. 'Fuck it!' As I spoke, I pulled out, went round the security guards' car and took off, with Colin right behind me. I hadn't even thought about how – or whether – we were going to get away with it. Fortunately, they didn't follow us, and there were no more road blocks on the expressway.

There are lots of gray areas in Chinese law, which people interpret in different ways. Perhaps the main thing on our side that day was the fact that, whereas the military and the police take themselves very seriously, and it would have been extremely foolish to have attempted anything similar with them, people working in other types of security jobs tend not to expect anyone to take much notice of them.

Something else that worked in our favor that day was the fact that the security guards were driving a 1980-something VW Santana: they didn't even stand a chance of catching up with a couple of motorcycles that can cruise comfortably at 120-140 kph!

We did 140 kph for the next 2 hours, and made up a huge chunk of time before exiting the expressway, where the guy at the toll booth made a half-hearted attempt to stop us and then just shrugged as we rode around the barrier and accelerated away. If we *had* been stopped, we'd have been fined 100 RMB – about US$15 – which made it a risk worth taking to be able to do 280 km in 2 hours.

There was a funny moment in the afternoon when Colin and I and the support team pulled in to a gas station and six young girls who were hanging out there couldn't believe that four white guys had turned up at this place in the middle of nowhere. Ted told them that Colin and I were Hollywood movie stars – in fact, that I was Ben Affleck, who they hadn't heard of, but who Ted suggested they should look up on Google. Whoever we were, they wanted their pictures taken with us. I just hope we didn't damage any teenage dreams in rural Jilin Province.

We'd done 600 km by the time we arrived, in the dark, in Baicheng. After 10 days on the road, the Middle Kingdom Ride was turning out to be rather more challenging than I'd thought it would be. Getting caught in the floods had been difficult, riding in the rain had been wearying, and some of the roads had been bad – as had almost all of the drivers. However, I think one of the main challenges for me at that time was how much I missed my wife.

I travel alone quite often when I'm working, and I always miss her, but the knowledge that I was facing 50 days without her was really hard to deal with. I'd known that the big issue for me was going to be trying to stay on schedule and do all the filming and note taking without compromising our safety. What I hadn't anticipated was that everything else would be overshadowed by the deep, almost physical sense of longing I had for my wife.

We left the Sauna Hotel in Baicheng at 8.30 the next morning – day 11 – and had a really good morning, riding on new, paved roads, surrounded by rolling green hills and grasslands under blue skies in brilliant sunshine. It was the *other* side of China, which I'd wanted Colin to see. A couple of hours after we'd set off, we stopped at Ulanhot, a town in Inner Mongolia, to explore a temple that was built in 1940 and dedicated to the brutal but brilliant Mongolian emperor Genghis Khan.

China has the largest standing army of any country in the world, and it sometimes seemed that we were going to encounter every single one of its soldiers during our journey. We'd expected to be stopped at checkpoints at various stages along the way and at some of them, at least, to be met with suspicion, if not outright hostility. Even so, we were surprised by the extent of the military presence on Highway S303, the road that runs along the north of China and forms the country's border with Mongolia.

Eight hundred years ago, when Genghis Khan invaded, and subsequently, when the entire country was conquered by Kublai Khan in 1279, China's fervent protection of its northern border would have been understandable. Mongolia had more or less stopped being a threat to China when the Mongols were driven out in the late 14th century – although, judging by the military activity in the area, the Chinese still weren't taking any chances!

Before we left Shanghai, I spent hours studying Highway S303 on Google Maps and Google Earth. The road runs through some spectacular mountains and stunning grasslands and, from the computer maps and images, it seemed to be pretty remote and isolated. Sitting at my desk in Shanghai, I'd become fascinated by this part of our route and I was pumped at the thought of riding along it, despite all the logistical headaches I'd known would be involved. Now, as we approached the highway, we were about to find out whether my enthusiasm had been warranted.

Having ridden all day from Ulanhot, we arrived at the turn-off for the S303 just as the sun was beginning to sink behind the mountains, and were immediately stopped at our first military checkpoint. The young soldiers seemed surprised to see a couple of non-Chinese guys on motorbikes, and two more following behind them in a car, which I suppose was understandable. What worried me was the fact that their appraising looks weren't friendly, and I felt my heart rate quicken.

'The road is closed,' one of the teenage soldiers told us, waving an arm toward a completely empty stretch of open highway.

Colin and I stared for a moment in the direction he'd indicated and when we turned to look at him again, his expression was thoughtful.

'Not closed,' he said, raising his shoulders briefly in apparent acknowledgement of the inaccuracy of his statement, before adding, 'You don't want to go on this road. This road is very dangerous. It's better if you turn around now. Find another way. Go back.'

Again, he waved his arm, this time in the opposite direction, toward the way we'd come. Despite the note of dismissive finality in his voice, I launched into an explanation of what we were trying to do. Once or twice as I was talking, his eyelids flickered and I could see that he was at least a bit interested in what I was telling him. Then he shrugged again, as if to indicate that it would take a great deal more than an 18,000-km motorcycle journey around China to impress him.

When explaining failed, I began to plead with him to let us continue along the road that had become almost an obsession for me during the many hours I'd sat in front of my computer at home. I'd often imagined what it was going to be like when we got there, but I'd never envisioned the scenario that seemed to be unfolding now.

'Hmm, too dangerous,' the soldier repeated, nodding and then shaking his head, as if in bemusement at the wanton foolishness of anyone who would even consider venturing onto such a perilous road.

I felt like a petulant child, frustrated because I was being prevented from doing the one thing that, at that moment, I wanted to do more than anything else in the world. But this wasn't just about me: there was a team of people involved in this journey. I knew Colin was as anxious as I was not to have to abandon any part of our planned route, and I hated the thought of letting him down. It felt as though the full responsibility of trying to persuade the soldiers to let us pass through the checkpoint was resting on my shoulders.

I glanced at my brother, who was looking the other way, anxiously watching a young lad who kept waving his rifle in our direction as if to emphasize or punctuate his colleague's comments. And then, as I was trying one last time to plead our case to the seemingly intransigent solider, Ted – our driver and fixer – took over, explaining in fluent Mandarin what it was we were doing and why it was so important for us to be able to follow Highway S303 through Inner Mongolia.

Suddenly, the soldier shrugged again, smiled, and said, 'Okay.' I held my breath, not daring to ask what it was *specifically* that he'd decided was 'okay' in case he changed his mind.

'You can go,' the soldier said. 'But not tonight. Tonight is too dangerous. Tomorrow is okay.'

I couldn't believe what had just happened. My heart was thumping and all I could think about was getting away from there as quickly as possible, before any of us said or did anything that might make him change his mind again.

'What's he saying? What is it?' Abandoning for a moment his post as rifle-waving-teenager-watcher, Colin looked at me, his eyebrows raised enquiringly.

'It's okay,' I answered, repeating what the solider had just said and trying not to sound as elated as I felt. 'We have to stay at a truck stop tonight, and then we can carry on in the morning. In the meantime, they want their photographs taken with us!'

After we'd set out on our motorcycles from Shanghai, it hadn't taken Colin long to realize the importance of retaining an inscrutable expression whatever happened. Now though, I could see that he was suppressing a grin as he gave an almost imperceptible nod of his head to indicate that he'd understood.

The sun was close to setting and we were about to embark on a journey westwards along a road that was basically 350 km of nothingness – no towns or villages, no gas stations, no hotels, just emptiness as far as the eye could see and for many kilometers beyond. Staying somewhere for the night and setting out in daylight the following morning seemed to be a sensible suggestion. Taking the soldier's advice – and hoping that we really would be allowed to continue on our way the next day – we drove a couple of kilometers back the way we'd come and booked into a truck-stop guesthouse.

We were the only guests there that night, and at about 9.30, we were in our room when the owner knocked on the door and told us there'd been a phone call and the local police chief wanted to see us immediately in his office. I was instantly anxious. I thought everything had been agreed at the checkpoint when the soldiers and police had been friendly and, having stopped trying to divert us from our chosen route, had concentrated instead on posing for photographs. Clearly, something had happened to change their minds. There could be no other explanation for being summoned by the chief of police at that time of night.

As Colin, Chad, Ted, and I got into the car and followed the hotel owner's directions to the police station, we tried to guess what the problem might be and to prepare ourselves for the arguments that we were about to become involved in. We knew that the whole border area was under the control of the military, and that we could simply be kicked out at any time and without any explanation, if that's what they wanted to do.

The fact that the policeman who ushered us into the police chief's office seemed uncomfortable wasn't reassuring. I recognized the man sitting behind the desk immediately as one of the policemen who'd been at the checkpoint earlier that evening. He'd seemed like a strange dude – shy but very keen to have his photograph taken with us. Now, we shook his hand, and then listened politely for the next 40 minutes while he talked about his job as police chief and about the town. The two lieutenants who flanked him made repeated attempts to persuade him to let us leave, saying, 'Okay, okay. It's very late now. Let them go. They have a journey to make tomorrow.' But the police chief just lit another cigarette and ignored them, and we kept smiling, nodding, and trying to look interested in what he was saying, although, in fact, I could understand only about one-tenth of it, and even Chad and Ted, who are fluent in Mandarin, could decipher less than half of his complicated, meandering sentences.

I suppose the guy just wanted someone different to talk to, and perhaps to show his minions that he was important enough to click his fingers and summon foreign visitors to his office at any time of the day or night. Whatever his reasons, we were on the defensive, because we knew that, in China, different rules apply and that the police chief had the authority to do whatever he wanted to do. In the Western world, you have rights, including the right to defend yourself against the State. But in a small town in rural China, if the local police chief had taken a dislike to us or thought we were being disrespectful, he could have been self-appointed counsel, judge, and jury.

It was a potentially dangerous and very unsettling experience, and by the time the lieutenants persuaded their boss to let us return to our hotel and we'd hastily shaken his hand again and left, I was exhausted.

Day 10 (*23 August 2010*)

This morning we had a police escort out of town, which was really cool – and something else I've never experienced before. It was weird not being allowed to talk to any locals and being under house arrest at the hotel.

Then we hopped on a toll road, which isn't allowed for any kind of motorcycle. What frustrates me is that people aren't able to make decisions based on the facts they're faced with at a particular time. If the authorities just explained to the people who work on the expressways that the ban on small motorcycles,

---

three-wheel tractors, and other slow-moving farm vehicles is to prevent them clogging up the roads and creating a hazard to fast-moving traffic, they could make judgments to suit specific circumstances. It's the same thing with having to fill up our gas tanks with little tea kettles that are designed to be used by small bikes with small gas tanks.

When we were stopped by the security people – who'd laid pylons across the road! – Ryan told me to leave my helmet on and not say a word. As I don't speak Chinese and the guys didn't speak English, there was really nothing I could have contributed to the argument anyway.

At first, they wanted us to turn around and go the *wrong way* on the auto-ramp to get off the expressway. When Ryan said 'No, that would be unsafe,' they said we could get off at the next exit, which was about 25 km away. It was the stupidest thing in the world, because their car would have struggled to go at even 90 kph, so there wasn't much they could have done to make us comply with what they were telling us to do.

We did get off at the next exit, as instructed, but the other road was closed, so we turned around and hopped back on the expressway. The girl at the toll booth gave us tickets, which she isn't supposed to do, and then the guy at the toll booth where we eventually got off wouldn't allow us to pay – because we weren't supposed to be on the expressway in the first place!

In the afternoon, we were riding through beautiful farmland, it was dry, the sky was blue, there was no pollution, and the air was the sort of fresh you can smell. I could almost imagine I was back in Canada, although, paradoxically, it also felt completely foreign and different from anywhere I've been before.

It was a long day, and we had a lot of fun. We made up some ground and had a sense of having really accomplished something. Tomorrow, we hit Inner Mongolia. I can't wait. You can already tell that you're in a different part of China, because the landscape has changed and the people don't look the same.

Day 11 (24 August 2010)
I slept badly last night and when I woke up this morning in a crappy bath-house hotel, I felt like shit. The breakfast was terrible and I barely ate anything. So I was already exhausted when we set off.

The morning was okay: we were riding on good roads and the weather was nice, and I enjoyed the temple – I studied history with political science at university, and I learned about Genghis Khan and his incredible story. By lunchtime, we were starving. We pulled in to a place in a tiny town and while we were waiting for them to make our lunch, they gave us a room with four beds in it where we could relax. The lunch was perfect – and cost just US$15 for the four of us. I can't get over how cheap it is here to feed four people.

The afternoon was just beautiful. It turned into the sort of day I'd imagined we'd get on this trip and haven't had many of during the last 10 days. All the West really sees of China is its overpopulated, dirty cities, whereas the places we were riding through today were isolated, empty, and beautiful: every view around every turn in the road was more stunning then the last one.

We'd hoped to get further than we did today – at least 100 km along the China/Mongolia border – but at about 5.30 we were stopped at a military checkpoint and ended up being there for about an hour. The border guards were very pleasant and wanted to have their pictures taken with us – I still can't get my mind round what a big deal we are here, four white guys with a nice car and two nice motorcycles.

The guys at the checkpoint said, 'There's nothing on the road for 350 kilometers. It's a really difficult road. Just be safe and leave it till the morning.' As it was starting to get dark, it seemed like the right thing to do. So we stayed at a little motel and, while Ryan was doing his video diary, Chad and I went to a karaoke bar next door for a quick drink.

There were about 20 people at the bar – 10 girls on one side and 10 guys on the other – and when we sat down and got a beer, everyone looked at us. There are probably around 20,000 people living in the town and I doubt they ever see white people. The singing was *horrible*! They wanted Chad and me to sing a song, but they didn't have any English karaoke titles, so we sang 'O Canada' – which they seemed to like!

We only stuck around for about 15 minutes, and when we left, they were all rocking out on the really springy dance floor. It was like a grade-school dance – all the guys and girls separate and no alcohol; there was just fruit and tea on the tables. It was a hilarious and interesting insight into what happens at night in a tiny forestry town close to China's border with Mongolia.

At about 9 o'clock, we were in the hotel room when the owner knocked on the door and said, 'You need to go to the police station and sign some papers.' When we got there, we went into a room to meet the police chief – who turned out to be a guy from the checkpoint who'd been really keen to have his photograph taken with us.

I had no idea what was going on. The guy was talking and laughing and I was thinking, 'As long as he keeps laughing, everything should be fine.' It was a bizarre experience.

While we were on the road today, the thought struck me that I'd really quit my job and sold my house. For the first couple of months of not working, it just seems like a crazy long vacation. But it's beginning to sink in and feel like 'real life' now, which is a great feeling.

Question: What am I doing after this trip?

Answer: Whatever I want to do!

Chapter 9

The forbidden highway

When we woke up the next morning, Colin and I had similar mixed feelings of anxiety and euphoria. We'd been talking about Highway S303 for the last few days, building it up in our minds until we had high expectations of what it would be like, and I knew Colin was as eager as I was to get on the road. We were wary too, because we knew that however well things seemed to be going – or, for that matter, however badly – they could change in a split second. Over the last 11 days, we'd learned that the key was to expect the unexpected and approach every new experience and situation with optimistic caution.

The air was cool and the sun was shining in a clear, blue sky, and after eating what had become our standard breakfast of steamed bread, hard-boiled eggs, and Nescafe powdered coffee, we wiped the dew off our bikes and got ready to set out along one of the remotest border roads in the world.

At the checkpoint where we'd been stopped the previous evening, the soldiers were true to their word and waved us through without incident. A few minutes later, Colin and I gave each other the thumbs up and turned onto the S303, heading west, with our spirits soaring.

The road forms the border with Mongolia and is the longest single-lane road in the whole of China – 350 km of nothing. The only problem is that it's a military access road in a sensitive border region, and, despite the fact that being waved through the checkpoint had enabled us to get onto it, it is actually closed to travelers like us, so we had no idea what might happen the next time we were stopped.

The road began to climb almost immediately, and before long we were winding our way up through the mountains. We could see for miles and the view was stunning. Apart from some herders and the occasional truck, there was very little sign of human life – just lots of sheep, horses, donkeys, and goats. We'd driven about 30 km when we caught up with Chad and Ted. They'd stopped the support vehicle at the side of the road to wait for us and as we pulled in behind the car, Chad got out.

'We've *got* to get some footage of this incredible scenery,' he told us. 'If you go back down the road and turn around, I'll go up there.' He pointed into the mountains. 'Then I can film you as you drive up the road again.'

Hoisting his camera and tripod onto his shoulder, Chad crossed the road and walked about 300 meters back in the direction from which we'd just come. Stretching our limbs in the sunshine, we watched him follow an invisible upward path through the thick vegetation, in search of a good spot to set up his camera, and then Colin and I turned our bikes around and drove down the empty, twisting, switch-back mountain road.

A little while later, Colin and I had just pulled in again behind the SUV when the almost tangible silence that surrounded us as soon as we turned off the engines of our bikes was shattered by a low, echoing rumble and a huge green-and-black Humvee sped around the corner in a cloud of dust. When it stopped on the road in front of us, I looked at Colin and wondered if his heart was beating as fast and as loudly as mine was.

The driver of the Humvee switched off the engine and for a moment an eerie silence descended again. Then three young soldiers jumped down from the monster vehicle and, gesticulating with the AK47s they were holding almost casually in their hands, began shouting questions at Ted, who answered them in a determinedly calm voice. While the soldiers' attention was on Ted, I turned away, felt in my pocket for the walkie-talkie we used when we did drive-bys, pressed the button and muttered, 'Chad, it's Ryan. Don't say anything. We've got military problems. Stay where you are until I call you again.'

As the young soldiers continued to shout and wave their weapons at us, it suddenly felt as if my head was swelling inside my helmet. Dropping the walkie-talkie back into my pocket, I reached up with both hands to loosen the strap under my chin in an attempt to relieve my growing sense of claustrophia. Taking a couple of deep breaths to force the air into my lungs, I tried to focus my mind.

I'd always known that our safety might one day depend on our ability to talk our way out of a potentially dangerous situation, and I knew instinctively that that time had come. As I wiped the sweat from my hands onto my jacket, I was hit by the full force of responsibility for the welfare of the whole team. The young soldiers were angry, agitated, and deeply suspicious of our intentions, and I had a horrible, sinking feeling in the pit of my stomach as I realized that, this time, things might not be going to end well.

'What are you doing here?' The soldier who asked the question was clearly the one in charge – maybe he'd been given the role because, aged about 18, he was apparently older than his two colleagues. Without waiting for an answer, he added angrily, 'This road is closed.'

'The guys at the last checkpoint let us through,' I told him, in a voice I hoped sounded respectful. 'They said we just needed to hurry on.'

Chad was about 300 meters along the road, where he'd been waiting for Ted to go back and pick him up, and I knew he couldn't see us. Letting Ted take up the argument again, I walked a short distance away from the soldiers, turned my back on them, pressed the button on the walkie-talkie, and said, 'Get up into the mountains, away from the road, and hide until I call you.'

'What's wrong?' Chad sounded anxious.

'The military have stopped us,' I told him. 'I don't know what's going on. I'll call you when I do.'

I turned back to face the soldiers just as one of them waved his AK47 at us again, apparently to warn us to stay away from the car while he searched it. After he'd gone through the pannier bags on the motorcycles, he told Colin and me to take the cameras off our helmets. His nervousness was infectious.

When they'd finished their search, the soldier who seemed to be in charge said again, 'You are not allowed on this road. You have to go back.' In fact, what they wanted us to do was go all the way back to the town where we'd visited the Genghis Khan temple, which was about 200 km out of our way.

'The town we want to go to is 350 kilometers along this road, but we'll have to travel 900 kilometers if we backtrack,' I told him. 'We were given permission at the checkpoint to use this road. If you make us go back, are you going to pay for the additional gas? We'll have to buy three times as much if we can't go this way.'

Gas prices are a big issue in China; but I think I knew as I said it that our expenses would be of no interest or concern to the soldiers.

'You can't go this way,' one of them said again, shrugging to emphasize his indifference to our problems. And a few minutes later, we were being escorted back the way we'd just come.

As soon as we were moving, I spoke to Chad on the walkie-talkie. 'They're forcing us to go down the mountain,' I told him. 'Start making your way to the road, and when they leave, we'll come back and pick you up.' I didn't have any idea how we were going to do that, but I was absolutely determined that we weren't going to leave Chad stranded on his own in the middle of nowhere, carrying a large HD camera and tripod, which, should the military catch sight of him, would flip them from nervous agitation into full-scale hysteria.

What we didn't know until later, when we saw the footage Chad had taken of himself while he was hiding in the mountain, was just how terrifying it had been for him, not really knowing what was happening and having to sit tight and hope we'd go back for him.

At the bottom of the mountain, not far from the checkpoint we'd breezed through so cheerfully earlier that morning, there was a little hut at the side of the road where a guy was selling drinks and snacks to the few passing truck drivers. I pulled in beside it and as Colin stopped behind me, he asked, 'What are we doing? What's going on?'

I turned off my engine, took off my helmet and placed it carefully on the ground, slid my arms out of my jacket and draped it over my bike, and said, 'Just trust me, Colin. Stay with me on this.' Then I walked up to the hut and asked for three bottles of water.

I was still standing at the counter, holding the bottles in my hand, when a huge German shepherd dog suddenly hurled itself across the ground toward me, snarling and baring its teeth. It was less than a couple of meters away from me when its owner came running up to the hut shouting at it, and, by some miracle, the dog stopped. As the man pulled it away, it was still barking and snarling viciously and the incident left me shaken and feeling even more jumpy than I'd done before.

Taking a deep breath and trying to convey a calm indifference I didn't feel, I sat down with Colin outside the hut, opened my bottle of water, and began to drink it. Ted had also pulled in off the road, and when he got out of the car and came to sit with us, I handed a bottle to him. The soldiers in the Humvee had stopped too and I knew they were watching us.

'Don't look at them,' I told Colin and Ted. 'We'll sit here, drink our water, and talk. Let's just wait and see what they do.' And, for a while, they did nothing, except watch us.

'Let's call their bluff,' I said. 'I want them to think we're not going anywhere. If they really want us to move, they'll get out of their truck with their guns, tell us to get back on our bikes, and follow us out of the region. I'm not leaving Chad up there, but as long as the military are with us, we can't go back for him. So this is our only option.'

Ten minutes later, the soldiers left, and a couple of minutes after that, I called Chad and told him, 'Ted's coming to get you.'

Colin and I waited at the side of the road for another 5 minutes, in case the military doubled back, and then we turned our bikes around and didn't stop driving until we knew Chad was safely in the SUV and we'd put another 100 km between us and the checkpoint. I figured that once we were more than halfway along the road, it would be easier for anyone who stopped us to send us *on*, rather than make us go back. In fact, at the next checkpoint we came to, the two soldiers who were standing listlessly at the side of the road just waved us through without even stopping us. We couldn't believe it; I guess the checkpoint soldiers don't communicate with each other along that road.

A little while later, we were riding through dense forest when I pointed to a huge fence that was only just visible amongst the trees and shouted to Colin over the microphone in my helmet, 'Holy shit! That's the Mongolian border.' When we slowed down to get a better look, we could see two Chinese guys sitting on stools in the middle of otherwise deserted woodland, with their guns resting across their knees.

At the first checkpoint we came to when we were out of the forest, the guards *did* stop us. In fact, they were very professional, examining our passports carefully and asking us questions about where we were going and why.

'We're going to the next town,' I told them, pointing to the west.

'This is a no-stopping road,' the soldier said, handing me my passport. 'Keep driving until you reach the next checkpoint. Don't stop. Just keep going.'

There was a dirt track running up the side of the huge mountain that rose, like something manmade, from the flat grasslands behind the checkpoint, and at the top of it was what looked like a military base, from where there must have been an unimpeded view for at least 100 km in all directions. I saw Colin follow the direction of my glance and I knew he would be thinking what I was thinking – that it would take a disaster of epic proportions to make me stop on that road.

Quite apart from considerations of personal safety, I didn't want to do anything that might put our film at risk. We'd arranged for people to fly out to meet us at specific points on our trip and take what we'd filmed back to Shanghai. But we hadn't yet reached the first of those points, which meant that we were carrying with us 12 days' footage – our entire program to date – and I knew that if we were stopped and detained, it would almost certainly be confiscated.

That night, Ted was still in a minor state of shock about what had happened while Chad was filming in the mountains. I'd taken a gamble when the soldiers stopped us, because I'd sensed that they didn't really know what they were doing. There's some mining in that area, mostly coal, which is what the trucks that passed us going in the other direction were carrying. But there are no tourists. So whatever happened hadn't ever happened before, which meant that the soldiers hadn't had any experiences that might have prepared them for dealing with three white guys. And as they didn't have a plan and weren't sure of their ground, standing firm and refusing to budge had seemed worth a try.

So *that* was the legendary, forbidden Highway S303 – a stunning, remote road that runs through some amazing countryside, with very few local people, no gas stations, towns or villages, just the occasional yurt, lots of donkeys, sheep, horses, and goats, and a few military checkpoints. That was the day when I felt a bit like Christopher Columbus, as though I'd discovered uncharted territory on a road no white man had ever traveled before. Perhaps that's a slight exaggeration, but I did have an incredible sense of euphoria.

I was pumped, too, to know that Colin was seeing so much and having so many new experiences, and it was really interesting for me to see his reactions. Less than 2 weeks into our trip, I knew already that it was going to change me profoundly.

They do such a good job of building roads in China and, theoretically, the country is well positioned for adventure motorcycle riding and exploration. I just wish there weren't so many obstacles and frustrations, such as closed roads and the fact that bikes aren't allowed on the expressways. Our journey wasn't easy – the roads could be dangerous, the terrain could be difficult, and the bureaucracy was hard to deal with – but, at a relatively young age, I was living a dream that had become a reality, and I was living it with my brother.

Day 12 *(25 August 2010)*

Today was a long, long day. When the military stopped us, we were thrown into one of the most intense situations I've ever experienced and I was freaking out, for several reasons.

(1) If they didn't allow us to continue along the road, we'd have to backtrack about 200 km and then take another road that would add at least 2 days to our trip.

(2) They didn't know that Chad was in the woods, and although I couldn't understand a word they were saying, it was clear from their body language and from the *way* they were talking that they'd be pissed if they found out, and even more pissed if they discovered he had a camera.

(3) If they found Chad, they'd probably confiscate all the video footage we'd shot so far.

(4) Even if they didn't find out about Chad, they might throw us in jail anyway.

There were a lot of things that could have gone wrong, any one of which would have significantly altered the trip. We were very lucky that the soldiers left when we stopped for a break, and we were lucky that when the dog attacked Ryan, its owner managed to stop it biting him, although it was only just in time, and it really shook us all up.

Once Chad and the camera were safely in the car with Ted, it was a collective decision to continue along the road. After that, we hit five military checkpoints and passed through all of them, which was unreal in the light of what had happened earlier. It's amazing that the military guys don't talk to each other. The soldiers who escorted us off the mountain obviously didn't contact any of the checkpoints – not the one behind us to let them know we were supposed to be going back and getting off the road, or the one ahead to say that if they saw us, they should send us back, at the very least.

I've lived my whole life obeying laws and being afraid of the consequences if I didn't, and here I am in an intensely communist country, blatantly disobeying military orders! I've said before that every day brings a new experience, and that was today's; it was also one of the most insane experiences of my life.

The logic behind what we did was that the border guards have no interest in creating a big deal by arresting foreigners, so the worst that would probably happen would be that they'd escort us off the road again. It was worth taking that risk, because we ended up riding 350 km through stunningly beautiful, completely isolated landscape – instead of having to backtrack and go almost 1000 km to get to where we ended up today.

This morning, I was catapulted into the most potentially stressful situation of my entire life, and this afternoon, I felt more isolated than I've ever felt in my life. We must have gone about 300 km today without seeing any towns, restaurants, or gas stations; there were just a few yurts, some tiny farmhouses, and an enormous number of goats, horses, and sheep. The sky was clear blue, the sun was shining, and it was like riding through a beautiful painting.

Chapter 10

The 1000-km traffic jam

The next day, we did 825 km on the bikes. The landscape changed from green grassland to desert and then back to grassland, and the road got bigger and better. We'd already done 500 km by lunchtime, and were averaging a speed of about 100 kph. We took some great film footage, and then basically just put our heads down and kept riding. In fact, the only thing of any note that happened that day was when I lost it at a gas station because it took us 40 minutes to fill up the bikes using a bucket.

It was dark and cold when we arrived late that night at a yurt-village resort in Huitengxile, which is in the grasslands of Inner Mongolia and home to one of China's largest wind farms. Despite the surrealism inherent in spending the night in a yurt in the middle of what would naturally have been silent, remote Inner Mongolian countryside, listening to the occupants of some of the other yurts drinking and doing very loud karaoke, we were creating memories that I knew would last a lifetime.

The next morning, Colin and I enjoyed some of the best off-road motorcycling we'd ever done. We loosened the suspension on our bikes, reduced the tire pressure, and rode out of the village and up through the wind turbines. Then we left the grasslands behind us and got back on the highway. We'd only planned to do a little more than 100 km that day – to Hohhot, the provincial capital of Inner Mongolia, which would mark the end of the first part of our trip – but almost immediately after we hit the highway, we ran into a long queue of trucks that were parked on the road.

It was the second time in 14 days that we'd been caught up in a news story. We had iPhones, and when I checked Reuters and the BBC the previous evening – as I did every night – I'd seen that there was a traffic jam stretching for 80 km from Beijing. Hohhot is about 500 km from Beijing by the shortest direct route, so the traffic jam wasn't going to affect us – at least, it wouldn't have done if the true extent had been 80 km, as mentioned on the news. In reality, however, traffic was being affected for a distance of at least 1000 km.

Even so, it shouldn't have been a major issue for us, because the traffic involved was attempting to go east to Beijing, whereas we were heading west. The problem was that as the more impatient of the truck drivers had tried to overtake the stationary line of vehicles by pulling out into the westbound lane, they'd successfully blocked almost any movement for all the cars that had been going in the same direction as we were.

I have never seen traffic like it. Some of the truck drivers had been stuck there for *several days* and were likely to remain trapped in that particular 50-km stretch of gridlock for another 4 days, or even longer. It wasn't surprising that some of them were losing their temper; what was far more surprising was the fact that most of them were just sitting there, accepting the way things were and not even trying to do anything about it. With that volume of vehicles, you only need one driver to do something stupid to bring everything to a standstill – and there were hundreds of them doing a whole range of stupid things.

It would have been fairly easy for Colin and me to force a way through on our bikes, but that would have meant leaving Chad and Ted behind in the car. So we took off our helmets and jackets and became motorcycle traffic cops, attempting to get the drivers to make enough space to allow the trucks that were on the wrong side of the road to move back into the eastbound lane, so that at least the westbound traffic could get moving again. Once the SUV was able to push through, other cars followed it, and Colin and I ended up directing a small convoy that was led by Ted. Then, as people began to realize what we were doing, more drivers got out of their cars to direct more trucks out of the way, and it became a team effort.

The whole thing was frustrating and exhausting, and a clear illustration of one of the many contrasts in China: you can wake up in the morning to the sound of roosters and goats and breathe the clean, fresh air of the empty grasslands; and then, within less than an hour, you can be dirty, sweaty, and angry, on a gridlocked road where a line of stationary trucks stretches further than the eye can see. It took us more than 4 hours to travel 60 km on that lost-forever morning.

We'd decided before we set out on the Middle Kingdom Ride that we'd stay at good hotels every couple of weeks, so that we could relax and do some laundry. Luckily, the day of the 1000-km traffic jam was the day when we'd planned to stay at a decent hotel in Hohhot.

The hotel's general manager must have heard the sound of our bike engines, because by the time we'd turned them off, he'd come out of the building and was walking toward us. I wasn't in the mood for the usual argument about where we were going to park the bikes overnight. But, to my surprise, he greeted us warmly, told us, 'Your bikes are great,' and gave us a couple of really nice, upgraded, rooms.

Although we'd planned to spend just one day in Hohhot, we ended up staying there for two, resting, doing our laundry and some basic repairs to the bikes, going through our film footage, eating pizzas, and drinking beers. In fact, during those couple of days we barely left the hotel.

We'd traveled 4480 km, we were about a quarter of the way through our journey – in terms of both time and distance – and we'd come to the end of the first part of it. Taking our film with him, Ted left us in Hohhot to drive his SUV back to Shanghai – via a southerly route, so that he missed the never-ending traffic jam. We were sorry to see him go, and at the same time hugely relieved to know that the first 14 days of filming would now be safe.

Our new driver – a friend of mine called Abdul who lives in Kashgar and speaks the dialect of that part of western China – drove to Hohhot to meet us and, on day 17, we began the next part of our adventure.

Day 14 *(27 August 2010)*

Yesterday was by far my longest day's ride ever, in terms of kilometers. We stopped for gas four times, which involved a lot of pouring from a teapot, and ended up sleeping 2000 meters above sea level at a sort of 'yurt hotel' in the mountains, which was a cool experience. It was very cold in the middle of the night, although, with four people sleeping in a single yurt, we were pretty cozy.

I *really* enjoyed riding off-road with my brother this morning. For most of the time we've been in Inner Mongolia, it hasn't felt like China; it certainly isn't anything like the part of China I knew, which is dirty, polluted, and overpopulated, whereas this area is isolated and beautiful, and there's really nothing here except nature.

We got on the road at about 11 o'clock this morning, thinking we'd reach Hohhot around lunchtime – which didn't happen. This afternoon was ridiculous. When we heard on the news that people were stuck in a traffic jam heading east to Beijing, we had no idea that it would

---

affect westbound traffic too. A journey that should have taken us an hour took us nearer five.

What was almost as shocking as the traffic jam itself was the fact that there wasn't one single traffic cop there. On our bikes, Ryan and I were able to get to the front of the line of trucks, figure out what the problem was, and try to solve it.

Those truck drivers, who've already been stuck in that traffic jam for *days*, could be there for as much as another week. In the West, time is one of our most valued commodities: everyone wants more time and everyone's always looking for ways to get it. Just think about someone in the West spending a whole week in a traffic jam – eating and sleeping in their car and using the side of the road as their washroom. I can't even imagine it. I cannot get over what I witnessed today. You'd have to put every single driver in Canada on one road and tell them all to go in the same direction to get that sort of gridlock there.

I don't even know what to say!

Chapter 11

Time out

After 3 nights in Hohhot, we were back on the road. On day 17 we covered 421 km in 6 hours, through landscape that changed from lush grassland to barren gravel plains as we reached the edge of the southern Gobi Desert. And as the scenery changed, so did the faces of the local people. For the last few days, we'd seen mostly Mongols, who look very different from the majority Han Chinese; now, we were heading into north-western China and the provinces of Gansu and Xinjiang, where there are large Muslim communities with ethnic roots in Eastern and Central Asia.

We'd already seen and experienced so much that it felt as though we'd been on the road for months rather than less than 3 weeks. Each of the challenges we'd faced had given us more confidence in our own abilities, as well as in our ability to work together as a team. The journey so far had sometimes been hard, but it had always been rewarding, and I knew that as the landscapes and the people we encountered continued to change, Colin and I would change and grow too: we were learning more about ourselves with every new test we faced along the way.

By the end of the next day, I was shattered and the buoyant optimism I'd felt as we left Hohhot was struggling to keep afloat. The day after that, the last day of August, we headed west across the southern Gobi Desert and did a lot of off-road riding. Although we hadn't planned to ride off-road, we were more or less forced off the highway by the huge amount of road construction that was taking place. So we let some air out of our tires, loosened up the suspension on our bikes, and avoided the road all day. It was tough going, but we had a good day – and saw our first camels, as well as mountain goats, sheep, and the occasional herder.

I had my first fall of the trip on that day too. I was going pretty fast and all of a sudden I hit some sand that was about 30 cm deep and lost control of the bike. If you're going to fall, you couldn't really choose anything better than deep sand on which to do it, and the bike and I were both fine.

That night, we stopped at a rest stop in the middle of nowhere, exhausted after a day of challenging but enjoyable riding.

We started day 19 in the high-plateau grasslands of Inner Mongolia and ended it, 534 km later, in the desert in Gansu Province. Then, on day 20, we left the town of Zhangye early and encountered the aftermath of a car crash. It was a sobering sight, watching a police tow-truck pull a black Chinese-made Geely car out of a ditch at the side of the road, and it served as a stark reminder of how dangerous the roads are in China and of how careful we had to be every day.

It was pretty easy riding after that, and we arrived at our next destination – Jiayuguan – at about 2.30 in the afternoon. We'd traveled 1500 km in the last 3 days and we were halfway across China: I really felt that we were getting somewhere. As the grasslands gave way to desert, riding on the dangerous, overcrowded, wet roads of eastern China became just a distant memory.

While we were in Jiayuguan, we visited the last, western, section of the Great Wall, a massive construction of stone, brick, and wood that was built to protect the Chinese Empire and spanned almost 9000 km from Shanhaiguan on the east coast to Jiayuguan in the west, across the historical northern border of China. We also visited the fortress that was built as a military base in the 14th century, during the Ming Dynasty, on the Silk Road traveled by traders en route to and from Afghanistan, Tajikistan, Uzbekistan, and western China.

It was exciting seeing things through Colin's eyes as he began to understand what China is really like, and as all the Western stereotypes were broken down for him. Every country in the world has problems; China's might be different from those of many other countries, but there's a lot of good here, and I was glad to be able to show some of it to my brother.

When we reached Jiayuguan, we'd traveled 6000 km from Shanghai and were nearly a third of the way through our trip. After leaving there, we would continue to head west, to the Pakistan border, through north-western Gansu and Xinjiang Province, where the Muslim ethnic minorities are mostly Uyghur and Kazakh, with some Mongols and Tajiks – one of the legacies of the intermingling of races and ethnicities that occurred along the Silk Road.

The next morning, we rode through the desert to the town of Dunhuang, which is also known as Shāzhōu – City of Sands – and spent the afternoon exploring the sand dunes for which the town is famous, being tourists, spending money, and having fun. We rode ATVs (quad bikes), did a sort of tubing down some sand dunes, and then Colin and I had amazing flights in a motor-glider and looked down on the incredible sand dunes from above. In the evening, we went to the night market in Dunhuang, where we ate some excellent food, I did some pretty skilful bargaining, and we laughed and enjoyed ourselves. In fact, I'd got so used to feeling responsible for everyone's safety and well-being and for looking out all the time for any potential problems, I felt a bit guilty about how much fun I was having!

Day 17 (30 August 2010)
I enjoyed the break we had in Hohhot. The day before we got on the road again, I had a good workout and a swim; it was nice to spend a whole day off the bike. Being in Hohhot also reaffirmed for me the fact that I don't like Chinese cities. The countryside in China is

stunning and the small towns are great, whereas the cities are noisy, polluted, and overcrowded. I suppose you could say the same thing about almost every city in the world, except that in China the noise is louder, the pollution is worse, and *millions* of people live and work in every major city here.

I was excited to be getting back on the road. We took the freeway, heading west out of Hohhot, because we were afraid of getting stuck in the traffic jam on the B roads again. I hate having to sneak onto the freeways: it's impossible to relax and just enjoy the ride and it ruins my whole day, constantly looking over my shoulder and never knowing if the cops are waiting for us somewhere up ahead. But at least it meant that by 4.30 in the afternoon, we were checking in to a hotel in a town called Haggin Houqi having done 420 km.

We've got a new guide and a new driver who are both Muslim and don't look Chinese at all. I hadn't realized quite how diverse China is in terms of the ethnic minorities who live here and their different dialects and religions. Hohhot is very 'Chinese', and just 400 km west, the people look more Middle Eastern. This evening, I had my first Muslim meal.

Day 18 (31 August 2010)

Today was a long day without much food, which is never fun. When we left town, we hit construction and got lost – they block the road but they don't give any indication of which direction you're supposed to go. It took us a couple of hours to work it out, during which time we traveled about 40 km, which was frustrating.

Another thing I've noticed as we get further away from eastern China is that people are getting poorer: in the little farming villages we passed through today, it looks as if they have a pretty bleak existence.

The mountains here are breathtaking – they're easily the most beautiful of all the beautiful things I've seen so far on this trip. And at the top of the mountains is grassland, with lots of camels and mountain goats. Although the road was amazing today, there were giant speed bumps every few kilometers, so everyone was using the dirt road beside this perfectly paved road, which was kind of weird.

I was exhausted and starving by the time we stopped at the truck stop we're staying in tonight. It's actually a bit of a shit-hole, but at least the beds look clean.

Day 19 (1 September 2010)
We got up early today, had a good breakfast, and rode for the first hour or so through desert. When we stopped, it was completely quiet; there wasn't a single sound. The roads were good and we were clipping along at about 120 kph. And then the weather turned and it rained on us – in the desert! It rained off and on for a while after that, and the temperature dropped to about 13° Celsius.

There wasn't too much to see for the first 400 km of the day, until we started driving through desert mountains made of the most incredible red rock, which knocked the mountains we saw yesterday into second place as the most beautiful things I've seen on this trip. I really enjoyed the last 100 km today.

We've stopped for the night in a small town called Zhangye, which is at the foot of some mountains. I haven't seen much greenery in other cities, but in Zhangye there's a park and the streets are lined with trees. It's probably the nicest-looking town I've seen in China.

Day 20 (2 September 2010)

We were on B roads for most of today, with huge mountains on our left. We only did about 280 km, because we wanted to see the last section of the Great Wall. First, we went to the fortress in Jiayuguan, which was really cool, although super-touristy: it had been made into a sort of Disneyworld, like Changbaishan. Then we went to the Great Wall, where, in complete contrast, we were the only people, and after we'd hiked all the way to the top, we just stood there, looking out across the most amazing view and just chilling.

It was a good day.

Day 21 (3 September 2010)

I had the most fun today in terms of tourist attractions outside of riding. We got up early this morning and hit the expressway: I think we're going to become known as 'The Toll-Road Bandits' – perhaps!

We did almost 400 km in less than 5 hours, which was fantastic, and then the afternoon was unbelievable. I never knew before we set out on this trip that I'd be experiencing the sort of things I'm experiencing. First, we rented ATVs to ride through the desert; they only let you drive them yourself for a few minutes before your guide takes over, which was probably a good thing because there was a strong chance I'd have ended up killing myself. Then we rode down the sand dunes on inner tubes. It was *so* much fun; I felt like a kid again, tobogganing in the snow back in Canada.

After that we went flying – which was, for me, the highlight of the trip so far. They had three hang-gliders with small engines and a laminated notice board with a list of prices for the different things you could do and see. It was all in Chinese and we couldn't read it, so we picked the middle one. And then it was just 'Off you go'. It was ridiculous! In Canada you'd spend hours signing legal documents, whereas here you show up, pay, and go. There wasn't even a company name, and you aren't given a receipt – in fact, the guy almost forgot to give me a helmet! It was unreal. I was scared most of the time – the landing was the scariest part – and I loved every minute of it.

Tonight, we hit a street market, where we sat down with our guides at a Muslim stall, ate some good food, and relaxed.

It was another pretty cool day.

Day 02. The morning traffic is a mix of cars and bicycles on the streets of Funing, Jiangsu Province.

Day 04. Ferry officials try to decide how much money they should charge for motorcycle tickets for taking the ferry from Yantai, Shandong, to Dalian, Liaoning.

Day 05. Looking out over a small fishing community on the Yellow Sea just north of Dalian, Liaoning Province.

Day 06. Looking across the Yalu River in to North Korea from the comforts of our hotel in Dandong, Liaoning, China.

Day 07. Ryan (left) and Colin stand in the pouring rain as a bulldozer clears a landslide from the road near Huanren, Liaoning Province.

Day 12. The forbidden highway, the S303, runs along the border of Mongolia and China's Inner Mongolia Province. In many locations, the border is the road itself.

Day 14. Horses graze amongst wind turbines in the Huitengxile grasslands in central Inner Mongolia.

Day 18. This sign in western Inner Mongolia near the border of Gansu Province doesn't help Colin decide which road to take.

Day 20. A tow-truck pulls a car out of a ditch beside the road – a reminder for the MKRIDE team that, statistically, the roads in China are the most dangerous in the world.

Day 21. A photograph taken from a motor-glider high above the famous sand dunes of Dunhuang in northwestern Gansu Province.

Day 21. From left to right, Chad, Colin, and Ryan pose for a
picture next to the motor-glider at the sand dunes of Dunhuang
in northwestern Gansu Province.

Day 23. Colin enjoys a breakfast of bottled water and cookies on
the road just outside Hami, Xinjiang Province.

Day 25. Our motorcycles and tents sit side by side in the Turpan Depression, the lowest point in all of China at -154m below sea level.

Day 28. Prayers at the start of the festival to mark the end of Ramadan in the square in front of the Id Kah Mosque in Kashgar, Xinjiang Province.

Day 29. Colin (left) and Ryan pose with two Pakistani border guards in the bitter cold on China's border with Pakistan on the Karakoram Highway in northwestern Xinjiang Province.

Day 33. Looking south from Xinjiang Province in to Tibet Province in remote northwestern China. Somewhere in those mountains our G219 highway criss-crosses taking us south in to Tibet.

Day 41. The stunning Potala Palace in central Lhasa. What a site to see after nearly six weeks on the road.

Day 45. Looking out over the Yamdrok-tso Lake just outside Lhasa, Tibet. We followed this road as we headed towards Mount Everest Base Camp.

Day 47. Looking out over a small collection of prayer flags at Mount Everest Base Camp, 5200 m above sea level. This photograph was taken on what was one of the most exciting and intense days of riding.

Day 59. Enjoying the view of the karst rock formations along the Li River in southern China. What a stunning boat ride.

Chapter 12

The Turpan Depression

The journey we were on was taking a lot of crazy turns. One day we were sliding down sand dunes in Dunhuang and the next day we were slogging through a tough 400-km ride. Getting out of Dunhuang seemed to be difficult – until we hit the *really* difficult part, which was 100 km of road construction that became an interminable cycle of pavement, dirt road, trucks, dust; pavement, dirt road … When we did have pavement, we were cruising along through a no-man's land of desert, in relentless, crushing wind that seemed to be capable of knocking us off our bikes.

The wind wasn't our only meteorological problem: one minute we were watching a dust storm swirl toward us, and then, almost before it had passed, leaving us covered from head to toe in dirt and sand, we were squinting as we tried to see the road ahead of us through almost horizontal hail. In fact, the hail was too heavy to ride in, and Colin and I stopped at a partially constructed office that was being built for the new toll road. Some construction workers who were living in the shell of the building let us take our bikes into a little office and shelter there until the worst of the hail storm had passed.

The whole day was exhausting – first, trying to ride through heavy traffic and road construction, and then battling against the elements. Before we set out on the Middle Kingdom Ride, I hadn't expected the weather to be good every day, but I hadn't imagined that it would be as bad as it seemed to have been for a lot of the trip so far.

There's always an upside, however, and in this case it was the feeling that the hardships we were facing were making us stronger, as individuals as well as in terms of the relationship between Colin and me. It was good to be testing ourselves under those conditions – for what purpose, I wasn't sure! Everyone knows that adventures aren't supposed to be easy; I just hoped we'd prove equal to whatever challenges lay ahead. However, there *was* one thing, perhaps above all else, that I was beginning to have serious doubts about, and that was whether my hair and my long, increasingly unkempt beard would be able to stand up to much more sand, dirt, diesel fumes, sweat, and wind!

The next day – day 23 – proved to be typical of the whole trip until that point. We knew we'd be driving on good roads, so we left the town of Hami in Xinjiang Province a little later than we normally set out in the mornings, and almost immediately we encountered a dust storm followed in rapid succession by heavy rain. Again, the wind was intense, and having to battle for every kilometer was beginning to wear me down.

We were heading for Ayding Lake, a dried-out lake bed in the Turpan Depression, which, at 154 meters below sea level, is the lowest point in China and the third lowest point on the Earth's surface.[3] The Turpan Depression itself is an arid basin – possibly the hottest, driest place in the country – which covers an area of more than 28,000 km^2 and has an annual rainfall (of about 2 cm) that is exceeded by its annual rate of evaporation (potentially 3 meters).

Eventually, the weather conditions improved slightly, and then the support vehicle developed a mechanical problem. We thought at first that there was something wrong with the gas filter, but it turned out that the fuel gauge was broken and the tank was empty. We siphoned just enough gas out of Colin's motorcycle for Abdul to drive the car to the next town and fill up. Although it wasn't a major issue in mechanical terms, it took 2 hours to get it sorted out, by which time there was little daylight left.

Despite the delay, we did make it to the lake, but we had to do the last 30 km off-road in the dark and then set up camp and make our dinner in surroundings we couldn't see.

---

3   Number two is Lake Assal in Djibouti, East Africa, which is 155 meters below sea level; and number one is the Dead Sea, on the border between Jordan and Israel, which is –423 meters.

Day 22 (4 September 2010)

The weather today may have been the worst weather of the whole trip. Even when we hit the flooding in Dandong, the rain wasn't freezing, as it was today. It was about 800 km to the lowest point in China, and pretty much everything had to go right if we were going to complete the journey in the 2 days we'd allotted for it. Inevitably perhaps, a lot of things didn't go right, and we've stopped early at a place called Hami, because we're exhausted.

This morning, the weather was decent and the roads were terrible. Then, when we hit the border of Gansu and Xinjiang, the roads got much better and the weather took a turn for the worse. We stopped at a toll-booth area that was under construction and sheltered under some cover, and then, when the wind became stronger and the hail was being driven in underneath the roof, we rode our bikes behind the construction site and into a storage room/office, where four or five of the construction workers obviously slept. So, there we were, taking our motorcycles into what was essentially their family room, and they were really nice about it – they even offered us some food. We spent about an hour and a half in there, sitting out the hail and the sand storm and waiting for our support crew.

Less than 24 hours ago, I was hot and playing in the sand dunes, and today – within just a few hundred kilometers – the temperature was about 10° Celsius:

there's snow on the tops of all the mountains around Hami.

We're going to leave later than normal in the morning, because it will be extremely hot at the lowest point in China, and we don't want to get there until around 4 or 5 in the afternoon, when it'll be marginally cooler than at midday and we can set up camp, have a nice dinner, and relax.

I've never camped before, which is a bit pathetic, but it's just never happened. So I'm looking forward to it.

Day 23 (*5 September 2010*)

Today was fucking annoying, and extremely rewarding.

We left Hami at around 1 p.m., which was 2 hours later than we'd planned, because the support crew had to get a tire fixed and it took longer than expected. It was 15° Celsius and sunny when we set out, and things went okay for about half an hour. Then there was a sand storm followed by a rain storm and it became super-windy, so we were instantly wet and cold.

It was like that for about 3 hours, until we started to come down out of the mountains and it began to warm up and the sun came out. When we stopped to have something to eat, everything was back on track, and then the support vehicle started spluttering and they had to pull over.

The SUV usually does about 600 km on one tank of gas, but they'd only done 400. They've just had a new gas pump put in, so at first they thought there was something wrong with that, and they spent about an hour trying to fix it. Then they tried some other things, and we ended up siphoning gas out of my tank to get them to the next gas station.

By the time we finally arrived at the dried-up lake, it was dark and I was pissed. Then I started thinking, 'You know what? I'm so lucky. I could be sleeping where those guys were sleeping when we sheltered from the sand storm. I'm on the greatest fucking trip of my life. Just relax!'

Chapter 13

Highway S301

There are two main roads from Ayding Lake: one goes north-west from Turpan to Urumqi, and the other goes south. We chose a route between them – Highway S301, which runs through the heart of the Tian Shan mountain range and which would give us a chance to do some serious off-road riding.

After we left the lake, we rode through sand for 2 hours, and then continued over dirt and thick gravel as we wound our way up through the mountains. We'd almost reached Baluntaizhen, the town where we wanted to stay, when we were stopped at a checkpoint and told by yet another AK47-toting teenage soldier, 'Foreigners aren't allowed to stay here.'

It was getting dark, we'd been riding off-road almost all day, and we were virtually incoherent with fatigue. When the local police chief endorsed what the young soldier had told us and was equally adamant that we'd have to move on, it meant another hour and a half's ride to a town called Hejing. Exhaustion hit me like a crashing wave and I had a strong urge to lie down on the ground, curl up into the fetal position, and sleep. I was running on empty and I knew I couldn't carry on. But that's exactly what we had to do. For the next 90 minutes, Colin and I kept each other awake by talking continuously over our communication system, and somehow we managed to negotiate the potentially dangerous terrain in the dark.

We'd set out at 8 o'clock that morning, had ridden until 10.30 at night, and had covered just 353 km, almost all of it off-road. And we'd been traveling for 24 days. No wonder we were exhausted. By the time we arrived in Hejing, I was so tired that my video diary was little more than a series of mumbled, esoteric self-questioning. I knew Colin was as shattered as I was, and I began to wonder why we were putting ourselves through the rigors of such an intense trip.

Why had I wanted to do it? Was it to spend time with my brother? That could have been accomplished anywhere, doing anything. Was it to ride motorcycles? We could have ridden them anywhere, on nice, smooth, safe roads. Did I have some sort of disease that made me want to organize and take part in elaborate, immensely difficult projects? Why had I chosen to circumnavigate one of the most militarized countries in the world rather than, say, Hawaii?

There *were* highlights to the day, the main one for me being the sense of peace I had when we stopped for lunch and watched a Uyghur man rolling out the dough to make naan bread in an oven. Another was talking about motorcycles to some Uyghur men in a small village. And another was riding up towards the clouds until we reached a high pass through the mountains, 3300 meters above sea level, where I looked around me at the incredible view with an almost poetic sense of accomplishment.

On the downside, we had a lot of problems with dogs that day. We'd be riding through an apparently completely deserted landscape when they'd suddenly come running at us, snapping and snarling at our heels and chasing our motorcycles as they tried to bite our legs. Once when it happened, Colin almost got caught: I don't even want to imagine what those dogs would have done if he'd fallen. I knew it was a problem that would get worse as we headed into Tibet, because I'd seen it there before, and that really bothered me.

Apart from a small amount of truck traffic, Highway S301 is very remote. There are no tourists and almost no local people, just the occasional group of derelict-looking houses in a vast and otherwise empty landscape that gradually changes from desert to mountainous.

At the end of almost every day, I felt that I'd been a wimp for thinking the previous day had been hard, and day 24 set the bar for a whole new kind of hard. By the evening, it felt as though something had drained out of me, taking with it all my strength, resilience, and stamina. Spiritually and emotionally I was fine; I just couldn't imagine being able to sit on the bike the next day for another 6 hours, or for 10 hours, or however long it would take us to get to the next place we thought we wanted to go to.

Although I enjoy challenging myself, I'd begun to wonder if things were getting a little out of hand. Perhaps I'd made a mistake and hadn't properly understood how difficult the trip was going to be. Drawing lines on a map is one thing; the reality of translating those lines into miles on the ground is something totally different. Suddenly, all the uncertainties that lay ahead of us and all the things that, until then, had made me look forward to every new day seemed potentially insurmountable, and I was afraid that I was being beaten by the challenge I'd set for us. After I'd recorded my video diary that night, I barely had enough strength – physically or mentally – to lift my hand and turn off the camera.

Day 24 (6 September 2010)
Fourteen hours of off-roading! Every day there's some new 'most' – most beautiful scenery, most exhausting riding, most ridiculous traffic jam, most enjoyable experience – and today we did the most difficult, most tiring day of riding we've done so far.

Apart from when a car came tearing through our campsite in the middle of the desert at 3 a.m. and really freaked me out, my first experience of camping last night was okay, although I do see now why houses were invented!

It took us 2 hours to go about 60 km on the road up from the dried lake this morning. When we stopped at a village to drink some water, I could see for myself what a melting pot this area along the old Silk Road really is. There were only a few people in the village, and they all looked completely different. Later, when we stopped in a city to have lunch, *everyone* looked different from everyone else. If you'd randomly selected 50 people from any street, put them together in a room, and asked people to guess where they were from, China wouldn't even have been mentioned. None of them looked Chinese, and no two of them even looked vaguely similar. It's fascinating; I could sit and people-watch all day long here.

After lunch, when the support team realized that they'd used 50 liters of gas to drive about 150 km – a full 60-liter tank usually lasts them for 600 km – we bought a 20-liter can and put it in the back of the SUV, just in case.

We were in the middle of the mountains this afternoon when we came across a beautiful glacial lake, full of the first clean water I've seen in China. Last night, we camped at the lowest point in China, in the dried-up bed of a lake in a desert, and within 150 km we were in the middle of stunning mountains with snow-capped peaks. So another 'most' for today was riding through 100 km of the most beautiful landscape I've seen in my entire life.

We also rode through areas where all the houses had been reduced to piles of rubble; it looked like there'd been an earthquake and the whole place had been evacuated. Four times today we were passing some remote farmhouse when dogs appeared out of nowhere and ran at our bikes, trying to attack us. Once, when Ryan was in front of me, a dog ran out at him, missed him and then ran between us, and I almost hit it. When you're riding off-road and a dog runs at you, you either try to avoid it, which makes you wobble, or you brace yourself for impact with it. I didn't like to think what those dogs would do if I baled. It was really scary.

By 9.30 this evening, we were about 10 km away from the town we wanted to get to when we hit a military checkpoint. There was less than half an hour of daylight left, but they wouldn't let us go on into the town. Even when we offered to give them our passports and camp in front of the police station, they wouldn't budge. So our only option was to turn around and go in the opposite direction for 60 km, through twisting mountain roads in the dark.

Driving in China is dangerous; driving in China at night is very dangerous; driving in China at night on switch-back mountain roads is extremely dangerous; driving in China at night on switch-back mountain roads when you're exhausted after 12 hours of off-roading is extraordinarily fucking dangerous. But, somehow, we made it.

Filling up my bike with gas using a little teapot is an inconvenience and the whole operation takes longer than it should. I can live with that, and I get that rules are rules here. But the consequence of the military not letting us stay in that town could have been serious injury or death – and that's a completely different issue.

We're in a hotel now and we're beyond exhausted. I had a lot of fun riding off-road today, and no lasting harm has been done – except, perhaps, that I'm now terrified of dogs.

Chapter 14

The Silk Road

I was still tired the next morning, but I'd recovered enough from my mini-breakdown of the night before to be able to face the day with enthusiasm.

We traveled 400 km in about 6 hours that day, including stopping for a proper lunch, and at 4 o'clock in the afternoon we arrived in the market town of Kuqa, in the region that used to be known as Chinese Turkestan. Most of the people who live there are from a minority Turkic ethnic group of primarily Sunni Muslims. They don't look Chinese and they speak a local language called Uyghur. There isn't much mixing of cultures in Kuqa: the Chinese, who are the minority, live and work in the high-rise buildings in the new part of town, and the Uyghur people occupy the old town, where, in the narrow lanes, you see men in Muslim skullcaps and women, with their faces covered, walking down to the river to collect water in earthenware pots: it's like stepping back in time.

I visit the region four or five times a year, to talk to the local people, take photographs, and document the changes taking place there. I love it, and I'd been looking forward to sharing it with my brother.

After we'd checked in to a hotel and had showers, we wandered through the lively chaos of the market amongst the donkey carts, the noisy, bustling crowds of people, and the friendly stallholders selling melons, sweets, kebabs, pungent-smelling spices – in fact, almost everything you could possibly want or imagine ever wanting. We'd been following the Silk Road for the last 4 days, since leaving Jiayuguan, and in the market in Kuqa, the mixing of races that had taken place along it for hundreds of years became starkly apparent: it felt as though we'd left China and entered Central Asia.

It was Ramadan, so no food could be eaten or served until the sun had set, and while we were waiting, Colin and I played pool against a local hotshot at a billiard table that had been set up in the middle of the market. The guy basically destroyed us, much to the good-humored approval of the crowd of people who gathered to witness our humiliation. First, he beat Colin, then me, and then Colin and I teamed up against him and he beat us both. They don't see many foreigners in Kuqa, so there was a lot of laughter and hand-shaking and, despite our defeat, we were the stars of the show. It was a lot of fun.

There's a vast world beyond the tiny fragment that each of us inhabits, and going out into it is the only way to understand other people, their cultures and religions: you can't travel and have the sorts of experiences we were having without learning *something* from the interactions involved. We'd traveled 8000 km from Shanghai on a journey that was exhausting, exhilarating, frustrating, rewarding, scary, fascinating, and, most of all, a privilege to be taking part in.

Day 25 *(7 September 2010)*

We got pulled over for speeding today, and when we took off our helmets and the guy saw that we were white, he let us go. I still can't get used to that.

Apart from the speeding incident, the riding was pretty slow and low key, on mostly good roads through desert. When we got to Kuqa and were trying to find our hotel, one of the roads was closed for construction, so everyone was driving on the sidewalk – two lanes of cars. Can you imagine how much trouble you'd be in if there was construction on a main road in the US and you just drove on the sidewalk! That sort of anarchy is a weird aspect of a country where most things are very tightly controlled.

The highlight of today by far was the night market in Kuqa. My brother loves Xinjiang Province, the Uyghur people, and their culture. So it was nice to walk through the market with him and listen to him talk about it.

Playing pool with some locals was a lot of fun too. I considered myself a pretty decent pool player, until today. The pockets were the tightest I've ever played with – tighter than on a snooker table – and the table itself was wobbly. It's difficult to hit a ball really hard and get it into a tight pocket; it's even more difficult to hit it softly and get it into a tight pocket on a table that isn't level. (Does that sound like I'm trying to find an excuse for my defeat?) There were 40 or 50 people watching us; wherever we go we're the main attraction, and that's still weird to me.

I love the kids here: they're so innocent and unaffected by the outside world. They look directly at you, ask you questions, and laugh at you. I don't think they'd seen cameras before. When I took a picture with a digital camera of one kid and then showed it to him on the screen, he was blown away, and when Chad showed some kids the footage he'd shot of them on the video camera, they couldn't believe what they were seeing.

In the market, some people seemed to be sleeping right by their stalls, and there was a whole group of people sitting watching a television, talking and laughing with their friends and families, with their babies asleep under their chairs. They have hard lives and yet they all seemed to be content, perhaps because the focus of their lives is their family: people work hard to put food on the table, and if they can feed their families, they're happy. It's a stark contrast to what happens in the West, where we get so bogged down by bullshit we forget the main truths in life. If you walk down any street in Toronto, most of the people you see will look miserable.

It isn't as simple as that, I know: I'm sure that the people in the market in Kuqa have plenty of worries and anxieties. But there *is* something fundamentally different about their approach to life. I'm a foreigner passing through China, just like all the traders who traveled along the Silk Road for hundreds of years. I stay somewhere overnight and I'm on my way again the next day or the day after that. It's a great way to see a lot of places, just not a good way to *know* places. All I can do is take snapshots of what I see and draw inferences about what life might be like for people, whereas in reality you can't *know* what their lives are like unless you delve deeper.

I guess that's what my brother's doing by focusing on this region. He fell in love with it and is making a photographic book about it, so he comes back several times a year and sees the changes that are taking place. He has a real understanding of the people here, whereas I'm seeing Kuqa for the first time and I'm judging the book by its cover. Even so, coming here has been very rewarding and I've had a lot of fun.

Chapter 15

The city of Kashgar

We drove 716 km in 8 hours on day 26, mostly through barren desert landscape. We did almost no filming, because we were tired and wanted to push on to Kashgar and regroup. We'd reached the end of the second leg of our journey and we needed to rest before we entered Tibet.

The ancient Islamic city of Kashgar in Xinjiang Province, in the western part of China, close to its border with Tajikistan, is one of my favorite places in the whole world. I've been there probably 20 times over the last 5 or 6 years and I love its atmosphere and the people who live there – who, as in Kuqa, are mostly Muslim Uyghur people.

The next day was a rest day, which started off really well. We took the bikes to a mechanic to get the oil and tires changed and then to a car wash, from which they emerged looking brand new. While the mechanic was working on the motorcycles, a group of men and children gathered to watch, and as we interacted with them, I had a really good feeling about being there with my brother.

In the afternoon, we walked through the old town, where they're knocking down some of the buildings and replacing them with new ones – and, in the process, destroying swathes of Kashgar's ancient heritage as well as its architecture. The regeneration that's taking place is controversial. According to the government, the reason for demolishing the old buildings is because they're not earthquake proof. I know it isn't for me to judge what's happening there, but the changes that are occurring are regrettable in some ways. It seems a shame that modernization can't take place more subtly alongside preservation of the old buildings: although some of the old houses *are* being rebuilt, they're using new bricks.

Wandering around the old town was like seeing a microcosm of China today, with whole streets of houses being torn down and high-rise buildings going up in their place. That's something you expect to see in Shanghai, not on the Silk Road in Kashgar.

Some people are angry about the destruction of their town, while others are happy to be moving into modern apartment buildings with electricity, indoor plumbing, hot water, and all the modern conveniences that people elsewhere in China are starting to have. The danger is that when you knock down the old lanes, where people sit outside their houses, interacting with each other and watching the kids playing in the streets, you destroy the social fabric of that society. People lose their sense of community – you don't have a real community when you live in a high-rise apartment building, cut off from your neighbors. The same thing is happening in Shanghai too – in fact, all over China. The sad thing is that what's being destroyed can never be replaced.

In Kashgar, we visited the house of a woman who burns the hair off sheep heads and feet. That's her job, and she wouldn't be able to do it if she moved into a modern home, which wouldn't have the fire she has in her traditional lane house in the old town where she currently lives. So she's someone who's very averse to moving.

The whole country seems to be being pushed in the direction of progress and 'improvement', sometimes without much apparent regard for what the human cost might be. I think my brother felt the sadness of that as much as I did.

Kashgar has a long history, first as an important trading post for Arab, European, and Chinese traders traveling along the Silk Road, and later as a listening post during 'The Great Game' played out between Russia and Britain from the early 1800s until after the Second World War as they fought for supremacy in Central Asia.

In the West, we have every conceivable modern convenience and a good standard of living, so we have the luxury of being able to choose to preserve our history, although we haven't always done so in the way we do now. Maybe it's because of what's happened historically in their country that many people in China are so focused on looking forward to a better future and don't care as much about conserving the past and the ancient architecture as we do. Perhaps only the wealthiest Chinese – who are now buying back ancient artifacts from around the world to replace those destroyed during the time of Mao Zedong – can afford to be sentimental about their heritage.

The city of Kashgar contains the Id Kah Mosque, which is the largest mosque in China, and the tomb of Abakh Khoja, a powerful local ruler in the 17th century who's considered by some Uyghur Muslims to have a been a prophet second only in importance to Mohammed. One of the reasons we'd gone there at that particular time was because the next day was the festival of Eid al Fitr, which marks the end of Ramadan. Thousands of people were already pouring into town to celebrate the festival the following day, so security there was tight.

That evening, we were driving past the Id Kah Mosque in a taxi on our way back to our hotel when I leaned out of the car window to take a photograph. A few seconds later, a policeman stepped out into the road to stop us, told the taxi driver to get out, and then sat in the driver's seat himself. It was clear that he was angry, but I couldn't work out what the problem was.

'What's wrong? What's he saying?' I asked Abdul.

'He's saying that you took a photograph of his colleague back down the road and that taking pictures of police officers is not allowed,' Abdul answered, raising his voice to be heard above the policeman's loud, gesticulating annoyance.

'No, no I didn't photograph a policeman.' I leaned forward to look at the man in the driver's seat as I spoke, but he wasn't listening, and a few minutes later, we were being ushered into the local police station.

'This officer says that you took a photograph of another policeman in the street,' the police chief said, turning my camera over in his hands and looking up at us from behind his desk with a stern, but not apparently hostile, expression on his face.

I stepped forward quickly, before Chad or Abdul had a chance to say anything.

'No,' I told the police chief firmly. 'I did not take *any* officer's photograph. I was holding my camera out of the window because I was taking photographs of the mosque as we drove past it. You can check all the pictures on my camera; you won't find any of policemen or military officers. I *live* in China. I know that taking such photographs is not allowed. I am interested only in the mosque. We are tourists here. Go on, check them if you want to.'

It was a meaningless offer: the police chief didn't need my permission or anyone else's to do whatever he wanted to do. In fact, he had been scrolling through the photographs on my camera all the time I'd been speaking.

Despite my apparent calmness, my heart was racing, because I knew that although he'd find no incriminating photographs on my camera, if he decided to send someone back with us to our hotel room, they'd see all our video equipment and the footage we'd taken in Kashgar and throughout our journey, and then our entire project would be at risk. Colin and I had spent a very large sum of money on funding for the trip, and I knew that we were only a hair's breadth away from everything falling apart.

For a moment, the room was completely silent and I could sense that Chad, Colin, and Abdul were holding their breath, as I was. Then the police chief looked up from the camera in his hands, shrugged, and said, 'Okay, there's no problem. The officer overreacted. Just try not to point your camera at anyone. You can go now. Enjoy your stay in Kashgar.'

The police officer's nervousness and aggressive reaction were understandable, I suppose, in the light of the recent terrorist attacks that had been carried out by Uyghurs against Han Chinese in the region. The Han Chinese, who constitute the largest ethnic group in the world, and about 92% of China's population, run most of the businesses and wield all of the political power in the country, including in Kashgar, where they are a minority group.

A few months earlier, when we were planning the trip, we'd known that bureaucratic interference and confrontations with the police and military were likely to be the biggest problems we'd have to face. By the time we reached Kashgar, we'd already had several altercations that had left me feeling edgy. But that day was the closet call so far. We were halfway through our journey and I felt that I'd jeopardized everything we'd done and everything that lay ahead for us simply by taking a photograph of the mosque when there was a policeman standing nearby.

We weren't trying to do anything political; we just wanted to see China, have an adventure, and document our experiences. I felt angry about what had happened, and I felt suddenly exhausted, too: some people thrive on confrontation, whereas I find it very tiring. I guess the whole bureaucratic dilemma in China is the reason why people don't attempt to do what we were doing. It isn't all about problems and interference, however, and despite the fact that similar things happened a few times and they were frustrating while we were actually immersed in them, they paled into insignificance compared to the incredible experience we were having.

Day 27 *(9 September 2010)*

We had a day off today and I experienced what was probably the largest swing in morale I've had at any time on this trip.

I really enjoyed interacting with all the people who stopped to watch when we took our bikes to a mechanic: it felt good to be engaging with local people. The other great thing about this morning was walking around the city with my brother and listening to him talk about all the things that fuel his passion for Kashgar. He was in his element, which was really good to see, and I had *so* much fun.

Walking through the markets and the old part of town was like traveling back in time at least 100 years – or being thrown into the middle of a Hollywood movie set. It was unreal; there was *nothing* that was familiar to me in the old town.

Abdul took us to his father's house, which is made of mud, clay, and straw, and has a little courtyard. Seeing a house like that makes you wonder why modern architecture took such a completely different turn. The old houses are probably inefficient in terms of space and heat, but they're beautiful. In some places, they're tearing them down and putting up modern apartment blocks, and in some places they're replacing them with what are almost modern-brick replicas.

Are the changes that are being made intended to be a slap in the face for the people of Kashgar to show them that the Chinese Government is in charge? Or are they a genuine attempt to improve the lifestyle and well-being of the people, by improving their homes? They're interesting questions.

I don't have any argument with trying to modernize the houses to some degree, by providing them with plumbing and electricity; but what they're doing to those neighborhoods really is a shame. I'd be very interested to see what the old town of Kashgar looks like in 5 or 10 years. Maybe they'll have done a good job; it would be nice to think so.

Watching a woman burn sheep's heads and feet sounds gruesome, but it wasn't at all: it was an extraordinary insight into the life of someone doing a job I had no idea even existed. The woman earns 3 RMB per head and four legs – that's 50 US cents (about 30p).

In the cab on the way back to the hotel, a cop thought Ryan had taken a picture of him, so he radioed ahead to his buddy, who stopped the taxi, took all our cameras, kicked out the taxi driver, jumped into his seat, and wouldn't let us out of the cab while he talked on his cell phone, apparently to someone in the PSB – the Public Security Bureau.

Having grown up in Canada, a situation like that, in which we essentially had no rights, was completely foreign to me and I felt very uncomfortable. Being detained without any explanation doesn't really occur in North America, or in most other places in the Western world, and it's something I wouldn't want to experience again.

There are a lot of police and military around at the moment because it's the end of Ramadan and people are gathering in large numbers for the festival tomorrow. The Chinese are always worried about cultural events like that, particularly in a town like Kashgar, where there have been incidents and attacks in the past, apparently by supporters of independence for the Uyghur people and by people protesting about their lack of right to protest.

The PSB officer was actually very nice and polite, and when he saw that there were no offending pictures, he let us go. Even so, the whole ordeal left a sour taste in my mouth; I hate feeling that we're constantly under suspicion – I don't know what they think we're doing.

What happened today really shocked me. The strong-arm tactics of the military and the police and the total absence of people's right to protect themselves are the worst aspects of China. Being here really highlights for me just how good Canada is in terms of human rights and the rights of individuals. The almost casual lack of freedom here is far worse than I ever anticipated. Until it became so blatantly apparent to us today, I don't think I'd fully understood that the police here can do whatever they want. It felt like they could have thrown us in jail and we'd have been there until someone came to help us – which, although it might have taken weeks, would eventually have happened, because we're foreigners. Chinese nationals don't have any protection at all.

We were looking forward to taking some pictures and capturing what is a very special moment tomorrow morning, when everyone gathers at the mosque to pray. Now, it feels like a bit of a scary prospect.

Chapter 16

The Pakistan border

The next morning, we left the Chini Bagh Hotel in Kashgar before sunrise to follow the crowds of men who were hurrying through the narrow lanes on their way to the Id Kah Mosque for prayers that would mark the end of Ramadan. After fasting during daylight hours for a month and taking part in the communal prayers that morning, the people of Kashgar and the many others who had been streaming into the city from the surrounding towns and countryside would celebrate Eid al Fitr by feasting and visiting friends and relatives.

Colin and I sat out of the way at the edge of the square adjoining the mosque, watching and listening as the loudspeakers crackled into life and, in one fluid movement, maybe as many as 10,000 men and boys knelt on prayer mats and began to chant, 'Allahu Akbar, Allahu Akbar' – God is Great.

I'd seen Muslims praying before, but never in such vast numbers. It was an incredible sight and a moving experience, which seemed to link the present to the past and the men and boys in the square to all the hundreds of thousands of men and boys who'd gathered to say the same prayers at the same mosque over the last five centuries. It didn't feel like China at all.

When the praying was over, the atmosphere transformed almost instantly from devout to festive, and as Colin and I left the square and headed back to the hotel to help Abdul's brother, Armin, load the Land Cruiser, the dancing had already begun.

Kashgar is about 1000 meters above sea level, in an oasis surrounded by low-lying farmland and desert, and as soon as we were out of the city, we were riding in the sunshine through open countryside and small villages, where the festivities were well underway. We had to drive through most of the villages at low speeds, partly because of the cattle that were wandering on the roads, and partly because of the young Uyghur motorcycle-taxi drivers who often rode beside us, checking out our bikes before giving us the thumbs up and speeding off in clouds of wheelie-dust.

About an hour into our journey from Kashgar, the landscape changed and the road began to climb: we were on the Karakoram Highway, following another of the many paths of the ancient Silk Road. For centuries, the Silk Road was the main route for traders taking silk, tea, porcelain and other goods out of China to the West, and for Arab, Indian, and European traders of spices, ivory, wine, jewels, perfumes, and slaves, amongst other things. It was also the route taken in the 13th century by the Venetian merchant

Marco Polo, whose adventures were said to have inspired Christopher Columbus; and, more than 600 years later, by the British explorer Sir Francis Younghusband, whose extensive travels in the Far East, Central Asia, and Tibet had first stirred my imagination some years ago.

As we snaked our way through the mountains, we were stopped at the only military checkpoint we encountered on the Karakoram Highway. Because China shares borders with some unstable Central Asian countries – such as Pakistan, Afghanistan, Tajikistan, and Kyrgystan – the checkpoint soldiers are on the lookout for contraband being smuggled in either direction, and I'd heard rumors that, despite the heavy police and military presence along the border, an increasing amount of heroin was also finding its way from Afghanistan to Kashgar every year. So it wasn't surprising that the atmosphere at the checkpoint was intimidating.

Above us, in the mountains, we could see a military base, and there was a machine-gun nest on the roof of an adjacent office building. But it was the AK47s held in the apparently careless hands of the dozen or so prepubescent-looking Chinese soldiers that really made us feel uneasy.

Colin and I were carrying little on our motorcycles that would cause any problems – just bottles of water, a large bag of raisins we'd bought in Turpan, and some extra fleeces and base layers for the weather changes we'd anticipated. We'd already passed through enough checkpoints by that time to know that it was best to remove our GPS systems and put them in our pockets. Most of the soldiers we'd encountered didn't seem to know that they were commercial devices freely available in shops in large cities such as Shanghai and Beijing. and the last thing we wanted was for our navigation systems to be confiscated and/or for us to be branded as spies!

The bikes made it through the vehicle checks without any problems, and then the soldiers turned their attention to the SUV. Each time we were stopped at a checkpoint and the back of the support vehicle was opened, I had a horrible sinking feeling in the pit of my stomach.

'Those are hard drives,' we'd say to the soldiers who were picking through our expensive belongings. 'That's a video camera. Those are cameras for putting on the bikes. That's an audio recorder. That's another camera, for attaching to a helmet.' Tapping my own helmet to illustrate what I was saying, I'd try to maintain a neutral expression while the soldiers fiddled with our equipment and opened our sealed, watertight Pelican cases.

The same thing happened every time; it wasn't unusual to burn an hour or more at a military checkpoint. This time, however, we were in luck, because the soldiers weren't interested in our camera equipment. They were looking for weapons and drugs, and as we didn't have either, they waved us through after just a few minutes.

For the next 4 hours, we rode on smooth, pristine roads that twisted and turned through incredibly beautiful snow-capped mountains made of fire-red rock, past herds of goats, sheep, camels, and yaks. By the time we saw the high mountain peaks reflected in the green water of Karakol Lake, the scenery was becoming treeless and barren. At 4100 meters above sea level, we rode through a high pass and then began to descend again through a wide, fertile valley into the Tajik Autonomous Region of China, where the small farms that border the highway grow mostly wheat and corn, and where we watched a herder use slingshot to prevent his sheep from wandering onto the road.

When we stopped for gas at the Sinopec Gas Station on the outskirts of Tashkurgan, I thought at first that the pale-skinned, green-eyed young man who walked across the forecourt toward us must be a tourist, probably German or Scandinavian. In fact, he was Tajik – another descendant of the mixed and intermingled races of the Silk Road and a reminder of the remarkable diversity within China.

We'd ridden our motorcycles 9000 km from Shanghai and I suddenly felt that *I* had a link to the past and to all the other travelers and traders who'd journeyed along the Karakoram Highway over the last few hundreds of years.

We were staying in Tashkurgan so that we could buy the permits we'd need to visit the Pakistan border, which is as far west as you can go in China – the fact that we'd been traveling west for more than 20 days gives some indication of just how vast the country is. The border is a tourist attraction and a special military zone, just like every other border in China. There didn't seem to be any hard and fast rules governing access to it, so we wouldn't know until we actually applied for permits the next day whether we'd be allowed to visit it at all.

After a good meal and a good night's rest, Colin and I woke up the next morning excited at the prospect of riding our bikes to the highest border pass in the world. And then we looked out of the window of the guesthouse and saw the thick cloud and pouring rain. When it's raining at 3200 meters, you can bet your ass it's snowing at 5000 meters, and as we huddled over our coffee at breakfast, Colin and I discussed our options. Should we proceed as planned up to the border despite the bad weather? Or should we sit tight and wait to see if it was still raining the next day?

When we asked the owner of the guesthouse whether the rain was likely to persist all day, he just shrugged his shoulders and said he didn't know. So we decided to head for the border. It was a decision that resulted in what was probably the most physically arduous day of my entire life.

At the military checkpoint just outside Tashkurgan, one of the soldiers said, with a wry smile, 'In the rain, on motorcycles: it isn't wise.' But he handed us our permits and waved us through anyway, and we set off on what was to be a 260-km round trip. It was still raining and just 10° Celsius. Half an hour later, it was 3°, the rain had become frozen pellets of hail, and the temperature gauges on our bikes had started to flash a warning of the potential for ice on the road. After another half an hour, it was –2° Celsius and the hail stones were the color – although not the consistency – of snow.

I can't even begin to describe what it's like riding in a hailstorm at –2°, 5000 meters above sea level. Colin and I are Canadians and we do a lot of skiing – quite often in the sun and always below about 2000 meters. There was no sun that day; just a bitterly cold wind and frozen hail. Riding a motorcycle in those sorts of conditions is a supremely miserable, uncomfortable experience.

The visors on our helmets kept fogging up so that we couldn't see the road ahead of us, and our hands were so cold they were burning – the hand warmers on the handgrips on our bikes were only good to about 10° Celsius. Stupidly, we hadn't bought any of the really good waterproof clothing we'd seen in July at the shop in Germany, and as the wet seeped through our jackets and pants and turned to ice, we slowly lost the feeling in every part of our bodies.

We stopped several times, left our bikes on their stands with their engines running, and sat in the support vehicle for a few minutes, trying to get warm and dry our gloves. And each time, it took a bit more effort and determination to open the door of the SUV and step out again into the relentless cold.

We were about 4 km from the border when I pulled in to the side of the road, got off my bike, and managed to move my frozen fingers just enough to be able to undo the zip on my pants so that I could have a pee. A few seconds later, as I saddled up again, I accidentally hit the kill switch with my right glove and the engine died instantly. Swearing loudly into the icy air, I tried to start it again, but I knew from the dull click, click sound it made that the battery had died.

Colin had stopped when I stopped and he walked over to see if there was anything he could do to help. By the time he'd walked back to his motorcycle, his engine had stalled and died too. We'd come a long way to visit the Pakistan border and I was damned if I was going to get so close to it and give up. As our bikes clearly weren't going to make it, we locked them to a metal pole at the side of the road and climbed into the back of the support vehicle – just 4 km away from being possibly the first people ever to have ridden motorcycles to the highest border crossing in the world. I felt cold, dispirited, and very disappointed.

A few minutes later, we were standing on the perfectly paved Chinese side of the Karakoram Highway in a snowstorm, talking to a couple of friendly Pakistani policemen and looking at the dirt track that the road becomes as soon as it touches Pakistani soil on the other side of the border. It was too cold to stay there longer than it took for Colin and me to do a piece to camera and have our photographs taken with the border guards; then we drove back down the road in the SUV to where we'd left our bikes.

Colin's bike started almost immediately, but the engine on mine still wouldn't turn over. The hailstones were like rubber bullets, it was blowing a blizzard, and we knew it wouldn't be possible to do any repairs at the side of the road. When we tried to start my bike by rolling it in neutral for about 500 meters, the engine didn't even splutter. So we decided to tie it to Colin's motorcycle using some rope from the support vehicle. If he could pull me back to Tashkurgan, we'd be able to find a mechanic and, even more importantly at that point, get out of the vicious, freezing hailstorm that was beginning to affect our minds as well as our bodies. Tying the bikes together wasn't a decision we'd have made in any other situation – towing a motorcycle is dangerous in any conditions – but the road was quiet and we seemed to have few other options.

To begin with, it was going pretty well; the only real difficulty was maintaining a low enough speed when we were going downhill. Then Colin hit a patch of gravel and his bike veered off to the right. A couple of seconds later, I hit it too, and when my bike skidded to the left, I fell. I'd fallen in Inner Mongolia and landed in deep sand, and Colin had fallen and slid through mud. This time, I landed hard on gravel, hitting the ground with my right shoulder, then my head, and then my right hip.

They taught us how to fall during the training course in Germany and told us, 'Aim to hit the ground with your shoulders, because that's where all the padding is. Never put your hands down as you fall: if you do, you'll bust both your wrists. Just hit the ground and roll.' If you told ten people the same thing, maybe five of them would react correctly when the occasion arose; the other five would probably follow their instinct and reach for the ground with their hands. It all happens so quickly you don't really have time to think. Luckily, I did manage to hit and roll, so

I avoided any really serious injuries: my shoulders and ribs were badly bruised, but I hadn't broken my collarbone.

When the first shock of the impact began to subside, I rolled onto my back and brought my knees up to my chest as I tried to force air into my lungs. Abdul, our guide, and Chad got to me first. I can remember shouting to them, 'I'm okay, I'm okay,' although I wasn't entirely sure that that was true. The next time I looked up, Colin was hovering over me anxiously. A wave of pain seemed to flood through every part of my body and the effort of speaking made me wince as I told him, 'On second thoughts, bro, perhaps we should rethink this whole towing business.'

'I think you're right,' Colin answered, reaching out his hand to help me stand up.

Apart from some severe bruising and possibly a broken rib or two, I really was relatively unhurt, considering the injuries I could have suffered. But the fall had shaken me up, both because it could have turned out very differently and because our trip would be over if one of us ended up in hospital – or worse.

We'd left most of our equipment at the hotel in Tashkurgan, so the support vehicle was empty and, with some careful maneuvering, we were able to load my motorcycle into the back of it. After securing the bike with ropes, we set off on the long, despondent journey back to town, with Colin riding behind us.

It was another day of 'mosts', 'firsts', and 'worsts': I'd ridden the bike in the worst weather conditions – and at the 'most high' altitude – I'd ever encountered; I'd been the most cold and the most wet I'd ever been; I'd had the worst motorcycle fall I'd ever had; and it was the first time my motorcycle wouldn't start.

Back in Tashkurgan, we managed to get my bike up and running again by jumping it from Colin's, and then Colin rode it around town to recharge the battery. It looked as though the bikes would be fit to carry on the next day, even if I wasn't. Without the hail and the intense cold, it could have been the best day of our trip so far. Instead, we were back in Tashkurgan, in the hotel we'd stayed in the night before, my whole body was throbbing with pain, and I didn't know if I'd be able to ride back to Kashgar the next day, or even the day after that.

We were about to head into Tibet, where we'd be doing off-road riding that would be far more physically demanding than anything we'd ever done before. How was I going to manage with bruised ribs and an incredibly painful shoulder? After talking things over, Colin and I decided that all we could do was play it by ear. There was no way of knowing how I was going to feel when I woke up in the morning, so there was nothing we could do except wait and see. Despite ending the day feeling really low, as if I'd been challenged to my core, I knew that, in the morning, today would be yesterday, and somehow I'd have to find a way to put it behind me and bounce back.

Before we set out on the Middle Kingdom Ride, I'd hoped that Colin and I might open the way for other adventure motorcyclists to do what we were doing and to follow our route of exploration around China. After the day we'd just had, it would have been dishonest of me to say anything other than 'It's a really difficult journey.'

The next morning, the sun was shining and the sky was clear – is that fair, that the one terrible day we had was the day we traveled to the Pakistan border? My shoulder and hip were stiff and sore, my ribs were tender, and I could lift my right arm only just enough to be able to ride the bike. But I wanted to get back to Kashgar. So we left Tashkurgan early and set out again along the Karakoram Highway.

We'd stopped at Karakol Lake to drink some water and have a break when a local Kyrkyz woman approached us and started showing us seat covers, little embroidered felt purses, and other things she'd made. Like Tajik women, Kyrkyz women are beautiful. They wear headscarves, lots of earrings and necklaces, and have almost unnaturally rosy cheeks – the result of spending so much time outside in the wind and cold at high altitude. When we bought some of the handicrafts she was selling, the woman invited us back to her yurt, where she gave us food and yak tea. Yes, she wanted to sell us stuff, but she and her daughter and the friends who came to say 'Hello' to us were genuinely charming, friendly people, and interacting with them was a sweet, restful moment that provided us with a complete and very welcome counterbalance to all the difficulties of the day before.

When we left the lake, we pushed on and arrived in Kashgar in brilliant sunshine and a temperature of 26° Celsius, in time to go to the Sunday animal market. The market was full to bursting with horses, cows, sheep, mountain goats, camels, donkey carts, friendly people, giggling children, dust and noise. There was a man sitting in the midst of all the chaos shearing sheep, and lots of other people loading animals off and onto carts. The cost of a sheep, so I was told, was 1200 RMB – almost US$190 – which I imagine is a fair price, although I have to admit that I'm rather out of touch with the current sheep market!

The market was another good antidote to the events of the previous day and it was impossible not to become instantly absorbed into what was taking place around us. I couldn't wait to see what tomorrow would bring.

Day 28 *(10 September 2010)*
The ride this afternoon was spectacular. I've been skiing in high mountains before, but I've never driven through mountains like the ones we drove through today. I saw my first yak and had my first attack of altitude-related shortness of breath, at 4200 meters above sea level. It's strange to think that people live their whole lives up there, in such remote areas.

This morning, in Kashgar, I saw the largest group of people celebrating their faith that I've seen in my life. It was a very powerful experience. And then, just

200 km away, we were in the middle of permanently snow-capped mountains, witnessing a different type of power – the power of natural beauty.

We're crossing our fingers that they'll let us go to the Khunjerab Pass tomorrow, which is at the border with Pakistan and, at almost 5200 meters above sea level, the highest border pass in the world.

Day 29 *(11 September 2010)*
Today turned out to be the new worst day of the trip. I'm trying to comfort myself with the thought that the memory of how bad other worst days have been has tended to fade over time. I just hope today is still 'the worst day' after another 30 days have passed.

It wasn't very cold when we set out this morning, but it was raining and, before long, we were, quite literally, soaked to the skin. As we rode up the mountain toward the border crossing, the temperature dropped, the rain turned to snow and hail, and our clothes stuck to our bodies as the water in them froze. My entire body was soon encased in a layer of ice and I was colder than I've ever been in my life. When the temperature reaches –2° Celsius, the precipitation is a mixture of snow, frozen rain, and hail, and you're riding through it on a motorcycle at speeds of up to 80 kph, the word discomfort takes on a whole new meaning, and then quickly turns to abject misery.

It was frustrating and disappointing to have to lock our bikes to a pole at the side of the road and do the last 4 km to the border pass in the support vehicle. We'd done 120 km in horrible, icy conditions by that time, because we wanted to get our bikes to the Pakistan border, and they died just short of it.

The border was really cool. We met a couple of Pakistani military guys who spoke English and were super-nice – one of them had the most incredible moustache – but we were too cold to stay up there for more than 5 minutes before calling it a day.

It was pretty scary when I was towing Ryan's bike and he fell. He hit the ground hard and hurt himself quite badly. That was the lowest point of the whole trip for me. Afterwards, I was thinking to myself, 'What the fuck am I doing here?' Then I remembered that I came on this trip for adventure, and adventures always involve overcoming obstacles and tough days.

We put Ryan's bike in the back of the support vehicle and I rode mine for the next 80 km. I was so cold that I was almost crying in my helmet. I just wanted to get back to the hotel and have a hot shower, a stiff drink, and some food. Despite his injuries, my brother rode my bike for the last 30-40 km while I sat in the car and tried, without much success, to get warm.

Mother Nature can kick the fuck out of you, and she took a beating on us today.

Back in Tashkurgan, we left Ryan's bike for an hour or so, and when it still wouldn't start, we jumped the battery and managed to get it running. Now we'll just have to see what happens in the morning.

If this is what Tibet's going to be like, I'm going to be fucking miserable!

Day 30 *(12 September 2010)*

We managed to warm up eventually after our visit to the Pakistan border, and this morning we made our way back to Kashgar. Most days when I'm riding, I'm keeping an eye on the time or the kilometers to see how we're progressing, but on the Karakoram Highway I didn't care: I was looking at the beauty around me and just enjoying the ride.

We always jump at any opportunity to see a snapshot of how people live, and being invited into a yurt by the lake was pretty cool. It was the first time I'd tasted yak tea – which is made from yak butter and salt – and the first time I'd been in a yurt that was actually someone's home. It was constructed from a wooden frame covered in canvas and animal pelts, there were intricately patterned rugs on the floor, and the smoke from the stove escaped through a hole directly above it. The woman and her friends saw it as an opportunity to sell us more stuff – they were better salesmen than half the people who used to work for me! But it was enjoyable for us, too.

In the market in Kashgar, we got very close to the whole process of raising animals to be slaughtered for food. I was a bit wary about going and I wondered how I'd react to it. Although I'm not a vegetarian, there's part of me that would rather not see how it all takes place. Growing up in a city, you miss out on all that – the meat just ends up on your plate and you don't even want to think about how it got there. On this trip, however, we're constantly driving through areas of farming, seeing cattle being packed into trucks, donkey carts, and horse carriages; it's all going on right in front of our faces. In fact, going to the market turned out to be okay – and I got to scratch a camel's head, which, fortunately, he really liked!

Today has been a good day, much better than yesterday. But then, almost anything you can imagine that doesn't involve actual physical pain was going to be better than yesterday.

Chapter 17

The majestic highway to Tibet

We were riding south from Kashgar to Kargilik when we stopped at the small town of Yengisar, which is famous for the knives that are made there. I've been to Xinjiang Province many times over the last few years and 2 years ago I started buying the beautifully crafted small knives that most Uyghur men carry with them and use for anything from peeling apples to cutting rope. The knives have stainless-steel blades and intricately decorated cast-iron handles, and the highlight of that day for me was going to the home of a local man who makes them in his courtyard.

The man's wife gave us freshly roasted corn to eat and we watched while he and his son made molds out of soil and then poured boiling liquid metal into them to make knife handles. When the handles were set, he popped them out of the molds, cooled them, and separated them. It was a highly skilled process, and it was strangely moving to see how much care he took over every part of it. As we watched him work, I couldn't help wondering if the craft he practiced with such nimble-fingered dexterity would be passed on to the next generation after his son. Will people still be making knives in the courtyards of their homes in Yengisar in 100 years time? My guess is that they won't, which made seeing it that day even more special.

When we left the knife-maker's house, we went to the market, where Colin and I bargained to buy some knives. It was a good way to round off a really great day, which marked an important point in our trip, because we were about halfway, in terms of both days and kilometers, and had reached our most westerly destination. From then on, we'd be heading east, which meant that every kilometer would take me closer to my family. The thought of going home was hugely motivating.

But we still had one of the hardest parts of the trip ahead of us: north-western Tibet. For the next 3 or 4 days, we were going to be traveling on one of the remotest, highest – and potentially coldest – roads in the world, at an average altitude of 4500 meters above sea level. I'd never been on that road before and I had no idea just how tough it was going to be.

The next day, we were on Highway G219, the Kargilik to Ali highway, which runs along the border between China and, first, Pakistan, then India. The borders with both countries have been the source of disagreement since the war between China and India in 1962, which was fought, ostensibly, over disputed territory along the Himalayan border, but which was in fact the result of more wide-ranging issues that flared up after India granted asylum to the Dalai Lama in 1959.

Highway G219 is the only road through the region and because it's a military access road, we'd had to get special permission to use it. In fact, it was really just a dirt track, which was rendered an obstacle course by a series of huge, water-filled potholes. As there was no way of knowing how deep the water was just by looking at it, the support vehicle drove ahead of Colin and me and if the water in a hole reached to mid-door height on the car, we found a way to ride the bikes around it.

We'd set out in the morning feeling almost euphoric, and the scenery *was* incredible – magnificent snow-capped mountain peaks, fast-flowing rivers of crystal-clear water, and, for the most part, no sign of life except for some wild camels. We rode through two high passes, one at 4000 meters and one at 5000 meters, and all the time a cold, persistent wind blew thick clouds of dust into our faces and made the riding physically exhausting.

It's quite difficult to maneuver a motorcycle on sand and gravel and it takes a long time to brake, so we had to go slowly. In fact, we made *such* slow progress that we knew we weren't going to reach the town we'd wanted to stay in that night, and we'd only done 300 km when we stopped to camp near a river. It had already become apparent that we weren't going to get through Tibet in the time we'd thought it was going to take us. The road was much more difficult than we'd anticipated, and the mud that covered it on some of the high mountain passes slowed us down even more. A huge amount of work and effort has gone into blasting the highway out of the mountains; when they get round to paving it, it'll be an incredible road to travel.

The next day, Highway G219 began to seem like a road without an end, and by the time we checked in to a small guesthouse, we'd done only 200 km in 9 hours, most of it at speeds of 20-30 kph. We'd ridden through every type of terrain we'd encountered during the training course at Enduro Park – gravel, sand, stones, small rivers, dirt, and dust – except this time the stones were covered in treacherously slippery ice and the dust came in the form of crevice-seeking dust storms. If we hadn't been on the Enduro course in Germany, I think Highway G219 would probably have defeated us, or even killed us.

There are very few villages on the road, and those that do exist are there purely to service the military bases and must have no more than about 20 families living in them. All the villages are pretty much the same: just a one-lane road with a one-story guesthouse where any passing trucker can eat and stay the night; a garage selling spare tires and some other basic stuff; and, in some of them, a few shacks that always seemed to be empty and shuttered.

What made riding that day even tougher than it might otherwise have been was the knowledge that we were facing maybe 20 days almost exactly like it. We'd chosen Highway G219 for the very reasons that made riding it exhausting: because it was isolated, remote, and challenging. With difficulty can come great reward, and it was some of the most exhilarating riding I've ever done in my life. I loved waking up every morning not knowing what lay ahead for us that day, but by the end of day 33, I was physically shattered. As well as starting to feel the effects of altitude sickness, I was finding it difficult to catch my breath – and my hair was *ridiculous*!

The next day, we did 360 km off-road. China is all in one time zone, so the further west you go from Beijing, the later in the morning the sun appears, and we'd been on the bikes from 10 a.m., which is when the sun came up, until 8 at night. The scenery was breathtaking and it was an incredible day of adventure riding. We rode through high pass after high pass, climbing to each one along a twisting switch-back road, already anticipating the moment when we'd see the highway snaking ahead of us down through the valley on the other side.

The landscape was so dramatic that I wanted to stop my bike every few minutes and take a picture. Every day we saw things that were more spectacular than anything we could have imagined – and then the next day we'd see things that were even better. Eastern Tibet is famous for its rivers, western Tibet for its lakes, and we passed the green-blue waters of one glacial lake after another.

Colin and I were sunburned from riding so close to the sun, but when we stopped to have our lunch, the icy wind seemed to suck every last calorie of heat from our bodies. It was so cold that we dreaded having to pull in at the side of the road to fill up our gas tanks from the gas we carried in big plastic containers in the car. Every motorcycle book tells you to sieve the fuel you buy in middle-of-nowhere places, because it's full of impure additives, and our frozen fingers fumbled as we tried to insert the filter we'd made out of a green-tea bottle and a woman's stocking – sometimes it's the simplest, cheapest solutions that work best!

When you're riding off-road on uneven terrain, the back wheel of the bike slews and bounces all the time, and if you sit down, your spine takes every hit. So, to avoid the risk of breaking your back, you stand up and let your knees, hips, arms, and elbows act as suspension. After doing that for 10 hours, every muscle in your body is screaming, and when you get up the next morning and do the same thing all over again, a pain develops in your back and neck that's like no pain you've ever experienced before.

On day 35 – our third day of riding on Highway G219 – we did 354 km, which is a serious haul over that sort of ground, and Colin and I began to feel more confident about our off-road skills. It felt as if we'd been battling the road and were finally beating it. All the riding we'd done since we left Shanghai had required little more than an ability to navigate; whereas what we'd been doing for the last 3 days had involved a different level of competence. We thought we were ready to tackle the Dakar!

The next morning, we set off early on an almost deserted, dusty track that was only recognizable as a road at all because parts of it had been flattened by the few trucks that had already driven along it.

One of the problems in Tibet is that the sun is so strong there's a huge difference in light intensity between full sunlight and shade, and when you ride into the shadow of a mountain or a cloud, it's suddenly very difficult to see. At one point during the day, Colin came round a corner near a lake into the shade, hit some deep sand, and went down. Luckily, he was only going about 30 kph, and apart from hurting his hip, he seemed to be okay. If he'd been going any faster or there'd been oncoming traffic, the outcome could have been much worse, and it was another reminder of how dangerous the roads are.

With 30 km to go until we hit the town of Ali, the road suddenly became perfectly paved. Before leaving Kashgar, we'd loosened the suspension on our motorcycles and reduced the pressure in our tires to give us greater traction for off-roading, and as soon as we hit the concrete, we stopped to tighten the suspension and increase the tire pressure. After traveling for 4 days through 930 km of dirt, dust, gravel, sand, and icy water, we'd reached the end of Highway G219, and as we descended out of the mountains, the landscape changed to grassland.

In Ali, we checked in to a two-star Chinese hotel, washed away the ingrained filth under hot showers, ate a hot meal, and talked to our wives on the phone. Life seemed pretty good.

Day 32 (14 September 2010)

We had a great rest day yesterday in Kashgar, and today we headed east, toward Tibet and, ultimately, to Shanghai.

When we stopped in Yengisar today, we wanted to see one of the town's knife factories, which are actually rooms where seven or eight people work, rather than the assembly lines that the word suggests. It turns out that they make the knives in the winter and sell them in the summer, but a guy in a shop said he could take us to see a local family of knife-makers.

We went through a door off the road into the huge courtyard of the knife-maker's lovely old house, and watched as he and his son made molds for handles and then poured liquid metal into them. The whole family was very friendly and it was really interesting to see a process that has probably taken place in that same courtyard and many others like it for hundreds of years.

This evening we had dinner with our new Tibetan guide, Kalsang, who'll be with us from tomorrow. Our local guides have been excellent: every evening they've helped us gas up the bikes and get them ready for the next day; they're completely professional and switched on in their understanding of what we're trying to do.

Apparently, after riding about 100 km on tarmac tomorrow, we'll be done with tarmac for 10 or 11 days, until we hit Lhasa.

Day 33 (15 September 2010)
Today was awesome. It was the first day with the new crew and it went really well. We saw some military training and at the first military checkpoint we stopped at, we had the longest wait we've had – it must have been about an hour – while they searched everything. When they saw our cameras, we had to wait while a message was passed up the ranks to see if it was okay to let them through.

The first 100 km was pretty low key and then we hit roads that were worse than any we've been on – and scenery that was the best we've seen. We didn't get as far as we'd hoped today, so tonight we're camping in the middle of nowhere, 4000 meters above sea level, where just walking leaves you out of breath. And it's *cold*.

Day 34 (16 September 2010)
I barely slept last night. I don't know whether it was due to the fact that it was at least –10° Celsius in the tent or the result of having trouble breathing because of the altitude. At least we were dry. When we hit the road this morning, the temperature had risen to about –2°, and by the afternoon it had reached +15°.

Today was one of the most difficult day's riding of my life – again. The off-roading was hard, and perhaps the worst thing about it was that it didn't seem to be going to end. We did about 200 km in 6 or 7 hours. Sometimes, we had to slow down to let a truck go past in the opposite direction, and sometimes we had to ride through a stream or river that had spread across the road. The problem is that obstacles like that often come out of nowhere: you round a corner and there's sand or water on the road, so you have to stop suddenly. My back muscles are killing me.

We're staying at a little truck stop tonight, where a bed costs 20 RMB – that's about 3 bucks! There's no electricity until they fire-up the generator at about 8.30 in the evening, and there's no running water. But it's better than camping for another night in the freezing cold.

In the mornings, I find myself wondering why I'm here, and by the afternoons I'm loving it. It's sometimes hard to understand why people put themselves through arduous challenges instead of staying at home where they're warm and comfortable. For me, it's the adventure and the fun of days like today. Looking back on difficult things you've done helps you to overcome other challenges in your life because you realize what you can do when push comes to shove, and that you don't need to shy away from doing something simply because it's going to be tough.

Day 35 (17 September 2010)
Today was the third really hard day in a row. I haven't slept much for the last 2 nights, the first night because we were camping at high altitude and it was freezing,

and last night because of some crazy military guys who were partying, drinking, and playing cards.

When I woke up this morning, it was the first time on this trip when I was so cold and tired I didn't want to get out of bed. As we were leaving town, three dogs ran after my bike, barking and snapping at my legs. I saw some dogs last night, and when they were still there this morning, I knew they were going to be trouble.

We did 360 km off-road today, which is way more than I'd have thought possible. It was exhausting, and very rewarding. We were above 4800 meters the whole day, and the high altitude makes it even more tiring. On the upside, we had the sun on us almost all the time.

Despite the sunshine, it was so cold we didn't stop for lunch until about 3.30. We'd bought a chicken and some bread this morning and I sat down and ate like someone who hadn't seen food in days. The fact that it was windy and I was cold paled into insignificance in comparison with how hungry I was. I've always been quite a picky eater, perhaps because I've always had so much choice of food. But when you're really hungry, you eat whatever's put down in front of you.

When we entered Tibet today, the snow-capped peaks disappeared and suddenly everything was green. There was grass, which we haven't seen for a long time, and huge rolling hills. I never knew that kind of landscape existed outside of animated movies!

It was cold today, although not miserably, soul-crushingly cold like it was at the Pakistan border. So despite being one of the hardest days we've had, I loved every second of it. When we arrived at the hotel tonight, I really felt that I was in Tibet.

Day 36 *(18 September 2010)*
We stayed at a little Tibetan guesthouse last night. I didn't sleep very well again, perhaps because of the altitude.

This morning, the off-roading was really difficult because the sun hadn't risen above the mountains, so everything was in shade and you couldn't see the patches of sand and thick gravel. When I came round a corner and saw sand ahead of me, I misjudged how deep it was. When you hit 30 cm of sand, you're going to fall, although, luckily, I just bruised my hip.

This evening, we're in a nice hotel in the town of Ali. I'm about to have a shower and try to wash off some of the filth from the road – my beard and hair are thick with it. Then we're going to have an early dinner and go to bed.

The last 3 days have been the most isolated days of my life. There's no cell-phone coverage, very few villages – the villages we *have* passed have had no more than a couple of hundred people living in them – and very little traffic on the road; there are just apparently endless mountains and emptiness.

I love Tibet: the landscape is unbelievably beautiful.

Chapter 18

Breaking down

After spending the night in Ali, we pushed on along a good road to Lake Manasarovar, a fresh-water lake close to the Indian border at an altitude of just over 4500 meters above sea level. It was cold and very windy all day, but the roads were mostly paved and therefore the riding was relatively safe.

We stopped to visit a monastery, where an elderly monk showed us a cave where the living Buddha, who brought Buddhism from India to Tibet in the 8th century, used to live and pray and where there was a small piece of stone bearing a fossilized imprint of what was apparently Buddha's footprint. When we left there, we were going to have a dip in a hot spring, until the woman there showed us the filthy bath and the disgusting plastic bags we'd be wrapped in, which would have more than negated any good the spring water might have done us!

We stayed that night in a guesthouse by the lake, where a Bulgarian tour group was celebrating someone's birthday, which reminded me that the next day would be mine: I'd be 32. More importantly, the next day was also my wedding anniversary. The thought that I'd probably be spending the night in a truck stop in rural Tibet 6000 km away from my wife was melancholic.

The next morning, after I'd had an emotional conversation with Jasmine on the phone, Colin and I drove along the road beside the lake and then continued down into the grasslands, followed by Chad and Kalsang in the support vehicle. Sections of the road from Ali to Lhasa are being repaired and paved, and we had to take several detours, which sometimes involved riding through grass, mud, sand, and water for anything between 1 and 5 km. The fact that there were a lot of trucks doing the same thing really slowed us down. We were back in the civilized world – which, in Tibet, as in the rest of China, meant road construction.

In the afternoon, I came off the road into a lot of sand and my back wheel stopped moving. Maybe I used the clutch a bit too much, I don't know. Whatever caused the problem, the clutch simply wouldn't engage with the gears, even when Colin and the guys in the support vehicle tried to get me started again by giving me a push.

We were in the middle of a vast desert-like plateau, 4800 meters above sea level, and even if we'd known what was wrong with my bike, we weren't going to be able to fix it where we were. So we pushed it up onto the road and waited for a truck to come by with space on the back and a driver who could be persuaded – by the exchange of money – to give me and my motorcycle a lift to the next village.

I felt really low. We'd ridden almost 12,000 km from Shanghai, which meant that a third of our trip still lay ahead of us, and now it looked as though we might not be able to complete it. We put Colin's bike on the truck too, and as my brother and I sat in the back watching the passing of the landscape we should have been riding through, I tried to console myself with the thought that at least I hadn't broken down on Highway G219, where we could have been stuck for hours, at best.

The truck driver took us to a town called Gongba, where we offloaded the bikes at a garage. But our problems weren't over, because no local mechanic in rural Tibet has even seen an 800-cc motorcycle, let alone fixed one, and no one holds spare parts for large motorcycles. We'd taken a lot of spares with us – brake levers, and foot levers, and all the things we thought might need to be replaced – but it hadn't even crossed my mind that I might burn out my clutch.

Colin and I had agreed from the outset that we would finish the trip whatever happened. If the bikes broke down and couldn't be fixed, we'd buy Chinese motorcycles, and if those broke down, we'd continue on bicycles: we were going to circumnavigate China whatever it took. In reality, we both knew that traveling 6000 km on 100-cc Chinese motorcycles wasn't a viable option. Did that mean our trip was over?

Before we set out on the Middle Kingdom Ride, we'd tried – and failed – to find a BMW mechanics' course that Colin and I could do. Then we'd searched for a mechanic who would let us spend a couple of days with him. We were willing to pay whatever it cost, but no one seemed to want to help us out, which meant that we had no idea how to take apart the engine or repair a broken clutch.

Despite his own lack of knowledge about BMW motorcycles, the mechanic in Gongba was really helpful. Climbing up onto the bed of the truck that had brought the bikes into the village, he managed to take the clutch on mine apart, clean everything, and put it back together again. By that time, almost every inhabitant of the village was standing watching the proceedings with friendly interest, and when we lifted the bike off the truck to do some test runs and it ran smoothly, they all voiced their loud, unanimous approval. Although Colin and I were impressed too, we knew that the real test would come when we hit the road again the next day.

It sometimes seemed that we'd been battling all the way, particularly for the last 10 days. Perhaps it's true that what doesn't kill you makes you stronger, but I was tired, and it was time we had some breaks. Before I fell asleep that night, I felt that I'd come close to exhausting my store of positive mental energy, and I had to remind myself, 'We're on a great adventure. If it was easy, everyone would do it.'

Colin is a bit more switched on about the mechanics of motorcycles than I am, so the next morning we decided that he would ride my bike and I'd take his. I think I'd said in my video diary the previous night that we'd just had the toughest day of our trip – or perhaps I called it 'the most challenging'. I should have known better than to tempt fate in that way, because the next day was a lot worse.

We'd gone about 80 km when my bike broke down, and this time it was clear that it was finished, at least until we could get a new clutch. We found a farmer working nearby who agreed to take the bike on his tractor to the nearest small town, where we paid a truck driver to take it 100 km to a bigger town called Saga.

Colin was tired, so he traveled with my bike in the back of the truck while I rode his, until a nail went through my back tire and into the tube. There was a lot of road construction going on – they were in the process of paving the road all the way from Lhasa to Ali – so I suppose it was bound to happen at some time. At that particular moment, it flipped the day over from bad to considerably worse and, after loading Colin's bike onto the truck, next to mine, we drove the last 30 km to Saga.

The arrangements we made for what happened next might sound convoluted, but there isn't anywhere in the whole of China that keeps clutch parts for BMW motorcycles, so doing anything at all was never going to be straightforward or easy.

Colin called some people he knew in Toronto, I phoned my friend Andreas in Hong Kong, and we arranged for a new clutch and the other parts we might need to be sent via

Fedex from Canada to Hong Kong, from where they'd be carried in a backpack by one of Andreas's employees across the border to Shenzhen on the Chinese mainland and then by plane to Lhasa. When the parts arrived in Lhasa, Colin and I would do the necessary repairs ourselves – somehow!

Theoretically, it might have been feasible for the parts we needed to be flown directly via DHL or Fedex from Toronto to Lhasa within a couple of days. But, as anyone who has experience of how things work in China will know, they'd then have been stuck in customs for months, if not years, and when they were finally released, we'd have to pay a 100% luxury tax on them. So the tortuous route was our only real option.

In case the clutch coming from Toronto still got stuck in customs or didn't get through to us for some other reason, we also had help from Austria, where an amazing guy called Andy, who blogs under the name of Chinabiker, managed to source what we needed and arrange for it to be shipped to Beijing, where it would be picked up by someone he knew and brought by plane to Lhasa.

The double air fares were going to be an additional cost for us, but we had no real option, and we were extremely grateful to all the people who so willingly put their own lives on hold for a few days in order to help us. We did consider buying a motorcycle and sending my bike to Beijing to be fixed, so that we could continue our journey. Apparently though, Chinese motorcycles are water-cooled rather than air-cooled, which means that you have to stop every hour or so and wait for the engine to lose some heat, and as we didn't want a 60-day trip to become 90 days or even longer, it wasn't a viable alternative.

Once the arrangements to get a new clutch had been set in motion, Colin and I put the bikes on another truck that would take them to Lhasa, and then we went ahead in the support car. It took us 13 hours to travel 700 km and when we arrived in Lhasa, shattered and stressed, we found a decent hotel and fell almost instantly into a deep sleep.

At 4.30 in the morning, when we were woken up by a phone call from the truck driver, who'd just rolled into town, we got up, unloaded the bikes in the dark, put them in a secure parking zone near the hotel, and then went back to bed.

It was quite late in the morning when we woke up again. We'd decided that the first day in Lhasa would be a rest day, so we had long, hot showers and a leisurely breakfast, and then headed out to Barkhor Market.

Shoppers in the market – which consists of thousands of shops and stalls selling almost everything you could need or want, including knives, statues of Buddha and Mao Zedong, hats, shoes, and food – mingle with the Buddhist pilgrims who walk, night and day, in a clockwise direction along the street that encircles the Jokhang Temple, spinning prayer wheels and chanting sutras.

On our second day in Lhasa, we visited the Sera Monastery, which is dedicated to the Gelugpa (Yellow Hat) sect of Tibetan Buddhism and where, in a leafy courtyard, we watched and listened – with the help of a translator – to five lamas taking part in a debate. One man stood up and asked a question and the other men answered it, clapping their hands, shouting, and pushing each other in their eagerness to put forward their own points of view. The debates take place regularly as part of the study process for lamas at the monastery, and they're amazing to watch.

The following day, we visited Potala Palace, which used to be the main residence of the Dalai Lama – and the beating heart of Tibetan Buddhism – until he fled to India during the Tibetan Uprising in 1959. The palace is built on rocks on the side of a mountain and has two distinct and very beautiful buildings: the original white building, where visitors used to go to discuss political matters, and a later, red building, where the monks prayed. Despite being well cared for and preserved, however, the palace has the rather forlorn air of a museum whose function is to remind people of something that used to be.

It was good to have a rest and to spend some time in Lhasa, but the Middle Kingdom Ride was all about moving on, and Colin and I were already itching to get back on the road again.

The first clutch that reached us – after we'd been waiting in Lhasa for 3 days – was the one that had been sent from Toronto via Hong Kong. Now all we had to do was fit it! Neither Colin nor I had ever done any major bike repairs before and the work took us 2 days. We wouldn't have managed it at all without the help of the guys in Toronto who sent us pictures and told us what to do, and without the support and assistance we received online from the motorcycle community.

I did a search for 'F800 clutch' on a well-known motorcycle blog for adventure motorcyclists called ADVrider and, amazingly, came up with a complete DIY repair schedule. I printed it off at the hotel and when the guy from Hong Kong arrived with the new clutch, Colin and I put the pages on the floor beside us and followed the instructions step by step.

I wrote a blog on the ADVrider site afterwards, saying that my brother and I were circumnavigating China on motorcycles and that the repair blog had saved our whole trip. The guy who'd written it, who goes by the online name of 'Lost Rider', posted a response, saying that he'd seen our website and thought what we were doing was awesome, and that he was glad to have helped.

It was a real boost to feel that when we'd needed help and had reached out to people in the motorcycle community, they'd responded instantly. We blogged repeatedly about the trip while it was taking place, and it was great to know that people were actually reading what we were writing and following what we were doing. Without Andreas, particularly, we might still be in Lhasa today, with a dead bike, waiting for the clutch to clear through customs. He and lots of other people stepped up huge and we really appreciated what they did for us.

In the couple of days it took Colin and me to fit the new clutch and do some other minor repairs on both bikes, we made mistakes and had to redo some things more than once. Eventually, we worked it out and got my bike up and running again, and when the clutch from Austria arrived, we stowed it away as a spare for Colin's bike in case we ever needed it.

We'd originally planned to go from Lake Manasarovar to Mount Everest Base Camp and then on to Lhasa from there, which was a plan that had had to be abandoned when my clutch broke. But as we hadn't traveled more than 12,000 km around China to miss seeing Mount Everest, we were going to have to double back almost to the spot where my bike had broken down.

Despite the stress and frustration of the last 5 days, Colin and I left Lhasa in good spirits, buoyed up by all the support and messages we'd received from people who were following our journey on the internet and by the knowledge that we weren't traveling alone.

Day 37 (19 September 2010)
At last I've had a good night's sleep – if I wasn't loving Tibet, I'd be feeling pretty down by now. When we set out this morning, we were hoping to do about 300 km, and as almost all of it would be on tarmac roads, we expected it to be a pretty easy day. And it would have been, if it hadn't been for the bitter cold and total

absence of sun. Despite the clouds, the ride through the mountains to Lake Manasarovar was stunningly beautiful.

When we visited a monastery that looked as if it had been carved out of rock, an old monk showed us the cave where Buddha used to meditate, which was pretty cool. Then we were going to go to a bath house, which turned out to be the dirtiest, nastiest bath house you could possibly imagine!

Day 38 (20 September 2010)
Today was an exhausting, bad day. Again, I didn't sleep well – some people were up partying really late last night at the guesthouse. It was raining when we got up this morning, and then the sun came out once we were on road, and everything started to look better.

At one checkpoint, they told us that the road ahead was closed and we couldn't go through. Ryan and I just carried on and got through without any problem, but the guys in the SUV got stuck – a soldier took their keys. They did get through eventually, though, and it was after we hooked up with them again that we hit a really rough area of sand and Ryan's bike stopped working.

A mechanic at the next village cleaned the clutch plates and put them back, which seemed to fix the problem. The people in Toronto have been really helpful and when I talked to a guy called Graham, who's a mechanic there, he said that if you fry your clutch, it's fried: you can't wipe it down with an oily rag, put it back together, and it'll work. So he was quite confused by what had happened.

I've ended the day with a giant headache. I'm not feeling very optimistic about the future, not least because I can't really believe that it isn't a major clutch problem.

It's at times like this that I just want to go home, where things are easy!

Day 39 (21 September 2010)
Today was 100% worse than yesterday – which, despite all recent experience, I'd never have thought would be possible. For the last 48 hours, our entire trip has been in jeopardy and I was awake last night trying to problem-solve and work out what we can do.

What also helped to stave of sleep was the fact that we were staying in the dirtiest fucking hotel I've ever seen. Can you imagine checking in to a hotel room and finding there's shit in your toilet? And when you tell them, they say 'Flush it'! Can you even fathom that?

When I played around with Ryan's clutch this morning, I was pretty sure it wouldn't last very long, and I was right. When his bike stopped, we were stuck at the side of the road in the middle of nowhere. Luckily, we found a farmer who offered to use his tractor to take the bike to Saga – a reasonably sized town about 100 km from where we were. There was no other traffic on the road, so it was our only option. But with the bike loaded onto it, the tractor only went about 10 kph, so we got the farmer to take it to the next small town, about 5 km away – which took almost an hour – and then we found a truck driver who agreed to take it all the way to Saga.

I went in the truck with the bike and everything seemed to be going along pretty well until we were about 30 km from Saga and I had a call from Ryan, who was some distance behind us, to say he had a flat tire. I guess it's Murphy's Law: what can go wrong will go wrong. We went back to pick up Ryan, lifted my bike onto the truck, and now we're in Saga.

It seems shocking to me that BMW Shanghai and BMW Beijing can't source parts for BMW motorcycles. There's no inventory in China: places like that just don't carry stock; they told us it would take a month for the part we need to arrive.

After a lot of phone calls, Ryan and I and the support crew are going to go on to Lhasa and wait there until the new clutch comes, either from Toronto via Hong Kong or from Austria via Beijing. It's good that we've got two avenues, in case the plans for one of them don't come together.

With hard-working, smart people you can solve almost any problem, and we have those people here. So, hopefully, we'll work something out. Meanwhile, we're going to be staying in a nice hotel in Lhasa, which will be a treat, particularly after last night. If we have to wait there for 7 days for the part to arrive, so be it. I'm not prepared to abandon this trip with my brother. We didn't set out to do a half-circumnavigation of China – I don't suppose there's even a real word for that.

Day 44 *(26 September 2010)*
The drive from Saga to Lhasa was 13 hours of construction and off-road detours, with just half-an-hour's stop for lunch. It was exhausting and painful, and it was the longest continuous period of time I'd spent in a car in my entire life. I was glad to be in Lhasa though, and it was good to stay in a nice hotel, with soft beds, laundry facilities, and internet.

My first good night's sleep for several days was ruined when we were woken up at 4.30 in the morning to unload the bikes off the truck – trucks aren't allowed to drive through Lhasa during the day, so they have to deliver at night. I'd been worried about what state our motorcycles would be in, because the road was so bad, but, apart from scratches on the pannier bags, warped center stands, and a broken light, they arrived in pretty good shape, and we were in good spirits.

We had a great time in the market in Lhasa. My wife likes the fat, happy Buddha statues, and they had plenty of those to choose from! Walking around amongst so much history was really cool. What surprised me was the military presence: there are soldiers in full riot gear with machine guns or shot guns at the entrances to all the tourist places. They even have little bunkers. It's like an occupied city.

In the Sera Monastery we saw how they print the scriptures – the same way they've been doing it for hundreds of years; it was really neat. The monk debate was really cool too, although it wasn't exactly what I'd pictured. I took some politics and political theory classes at college, and as we listened to the monks arguing, I could almost imagine I was in the town square in the Republic, in the time of Plato or Aristotle. The things they were talking about were of a deeply philosophical nature, and I really wished I could speak the language so that I could understand what they were saying. After the debate, we went to the Potala Palace, which is incredible, huge, and definitely one of the things you really should see during your lifetime: it's that special.

What we saw today has made me want to read up on the Buddhist religion when we finish the trip.

When we knew what was wrong with Ryan's clutch and that somehow we'd have to get the parts to repair it, we talked long and hard about what our options were and it was really stressful to think that we might have to give up our trip.

When the new clutch arrived, we had a box full of bits of metal that we had to put together properly if we were going to have any chance of carrying on. I was nervous about fitting them, because I'd never done anything like that before. Although I'm probably marginally more 'handy' than my brother, that's more of a chalk-and-calcium-carbonate than a chalk-and-cheese comparison, so it was risky!

Our first attempt went wrong and the clutch didn't work, and when we went to bed that night, I was thinking, 'What the fuck's going to happen if we can't get this bike going?'

The next morning, Ryan found a really good blog online and we gave it another go. We fitted the clutch okay this time, but we couldn't attach it properly to the gear box, and then there was an oil leak. It seemed like every time we fixed one thing, something else broke. It was really frustrating, and it meant that we spent about 4 hours working on a job that should probably have taken only 1.

Now it's day 44; we've learned a lot and we've got two working motorcycles. Tomorrow, we're going to head back to Everest. I pray to God the bikes last. What do we do if they don't? We've come way too far to give up, but there's a limit to the additional costs we can incur.

After Everest, we'll make our way east through Tibet, then south, and then up the coast to Shanghai. Even though I've loved our trip, it's a good feeling to be coming to the last part of it. We left Shanghai a long time ago, and I'm really looking forward to seeing my wife again and to the prospect of going traveling with her for the next year.

What will actually happen in the next few days is up in the air. Because Eastern Tibet is apparently closed to foreigners, we don't know if we're going to try to go through it quietly or if we're going to have to do a huge detour to avoid it. There are still a lot of stresses ahead of us.

Chapter 19

Mount Everest

It was a huge relief to have two working motorcycles again and to be able to continue our journey. The fact that, in just 6 days, we'd managed to procure a part from Toronto and another from Austria and have them flown into Tibet and then Colin and I had done the clutch repair ourselves was a boost to our confidence. It was an unbelievable feeling to be on the road again. Lhasa is a good town, but I was glad to be moving on.

The first day on the road, we backtracked about 350 km west to near where we'd broken down. The road – which was paved for its entire length – twisted around the mountains, through a pass, and then down again to the edge of Yamdrok Lake at about 4500 meters above sea level. Riding beside the lake was the highlight of the day for me: the sun was out, the sky was blue, I was with my brother, and we were on our way to Mount Everest Base Camp!

After going through another pass and then descending 1500 meters, the rocky, glacial landscape disappeared abruptly and as far as the eye could see there were wheat fields and rolling hills bathed in the colors of autumn. We stayed that night in the town of Shigatse, and the next day rode another 300 km through countryside so stunning that, 6 weeks ago, before we'd seen so many other incredible landscapes – and if we hadn't been so keen to push on to Everest – it would have halted us repeatedly in our tracks.

We did stop for a while that day beside the 5000-km marker on Highway G318, which starts near my home in Shanghai, passes through Tibet, and ends at China's border with Nepal. In the 46 days since we'd set out from Shanghai, we'd ridden almost 12,400 km via a circuitous route; it was strange to think that, by the shortest, most direct route, we were only 5000 km from my home. We stopped again later too, when we came through the first high pass of the day and looked up to see the massive snow-capped peaks of the Himalayas spread out in front of us like some magnificent oil painting.

We bought our tickets for Everest Base Camp at a small town called Shegar and then rode for about another hour to the truck-stop town of Tingri, where we left the highway and continued off-road for 20 km to a small guesthouse in a farming village in the mountains.

Independent travel isn't allowed in Tibet, and tourism – including to Mount Everest – is strictly controlled, which means that to get through the many military checkpoints, you have to have a travel permit and a guide in an SUV. The tickets for Everest Base Camp cost US$30 per person and the SUV, which one of our guides was driving, was another $60. They said there was no charge for motorcycles, until someone went outside and saw our 800-cc bikes and decided we'd have to pay an additional $15 for each of them. In the greater scheme of things, even a couple of hundred US dollars doesn't seem much to pay for the privilege of getting so close to the highest mountain in the world!

The village where we were staying the night was in the shadow of some of the other spectacular 8000-meter peaks of the Himalayas, although not within sight of Everest itself. It was late afternoon when we arrived there, and as soon as we stopped, we were surrounded by laughing, chattering kids, most of them shoeless, one of them totally naked, and all of them covered in the dirt in which they'd been playing. It was nearing the end of the wheat harvest, and we also talked to some of the women who were turning stacks of wheat – in Tibetan culture, it's the women who do most of the agricultural work, and they work really hard.

I'd chosen a guesthouse for us to stay in that was off the tourist trail, in a place where well-heeled visitors in Land Cruisers are rarely, if ever, seen and where the local people lead lives that must have changed very little from those their ancestors have led for hundreds of years. We'd probably have parked our bikes in the courtyard of the farmhouse where we were staying, if it hadn't been occupied by a large, impassive, and, fortunately, uninterested cow.

'Do not touch or try to mount the cows,' the farmer told us – an instruction that wasn't strictly necessary and that made me wonder what might have happened in the past to make him issue it. Touching the cows certainly wasn't something any of us had been planning to do, and as Chad watched them meander in and out of the house, he came close to losing his cool.

There are few trees in Tibet and, consequently, there are few wooden buildings. The farmhouse was made of rocks and mud bricks, and the family generated power from huge batteries and cooked on a fire fueled mainly by yak dung. The ground floor of the house was used for storage and, in the wintertime, for housing animals, while the family lived on the floor above, which had an open living area and a dining area with a stove. There was a plastic skylight on the first floor and another in the bathroom, and the toilet consisted of a hole in the floor through which all waste dropped to the ground below, where it was left to dry out before being used as fuel.

That night, the whole family slept together around the stove in the dining area, and Colin, Chad, Kalsang, and I shared a separate room, where we slept in our sleeping bags on wooden bed frames covered with three layers of Tibetan rugs, in a temperature that fell to –19° Celsius.

When the women had finished their work in the fields, they cooked the evening meal and took care of the baby – whose parents I never managed to identify from amongst the different generations of extended family who were living together in the farmhouse. All the women had the same long, braided hair, large brown eyes, high cheekbones, and permanently bright-red cheeks – the result of working outside every day of the year in strong sun and wind.

Living and working conditions in Tibet are hard and most of the men and women look considerably older than their true ages.

The dinner we ate with the family that night consisted of an excellent thick soup made from noodles and yak meat, washed down with yak butter tea. Sunset came quickly as the sun sank behind the high mountains surrounding the village, and it brought with it a sudden drop in temperature. We had a big day ahead of us, and it wasn't much later when we went to bed.

I woke up the next morning to the familiar sound of dogs barking and the less familiar one of a baby crying in the next room. Still groggy with sleep, I raised my head from the bed just high enough to be able to look around and try to orientate myself. Colin and Chad were still fast asleep, so I lay down again, pulling my sleeping bag tightly around me to shut out the freezing air that was seeping through the opening, happy to defer for a bit longer the moment when I would have to unzip it and venture out into the cold. Closing my eyes, I listened to the sound of footsteps on the rooftop terrace above my head, and then I remembered that it was game day: the day when I was going to visit Everest Base Camp with my brother.

It was nearly 9 o'clock that morning by the time the sun was visible above the Himalayas. By 9.30, we'd eaten some freshly baked bread and hard-boiled eggs, drunk some more yak butter tea and nasty 'Gold Roast' coffee we'd picked up in Kashgar when we were there, and we were good to go.

The sunlight hadn't yet reached the valley floor when we set out, and although our hands and feet were soon frozen, our spirits were high as we followed the road out of the village and up into the mountains. It was one of the toughest off-road days we'd had – in fact, there was no road at all, just sand and loose gravel – but the arduous riding was more than compensated for by the breathtaking scenery, and as the sun rose steadily higher until it appeared above the mountain peaks, the temperature rose too.

It took us almost an hour to travel the first 10 km. We stopped several times, each time stripping off another layer of clothing as the temperature increased from 2° to 22° Celsius, and after another hour, we entered a dried-up glacial valley where the terrain changed abruptly and we were riding over ground that was covered with huge rocks, stones, and small rivers.

The higher the road climbed, the thinner the air became and the more difficult it was to breathe. It takes just 10 minutes to become light-headed and breathless when you're riding standing up over that kind of terrain and at that altitude, and we had to take frequent breaks to drink water and recover enough to be able to carry on for another 10 minutes.

The most difficult part of the day was negotiating a 15-km stretch of dirt trail that had been flooded by the icy water of a river that reached to wheel height on our bikes, seeped into our boots, and soaked our riding suits, and beneath which was a layer of dangerously slippery rocks and mud.

The closer we got to Everest Base Camp, the more traffic we encountered – mostly SUVs and a surprising number of bicycles, and most of it going in the opposite direction from the way we were heading. There was little room on the dirt track for two vehicles to pass each other, and Colin and I often had to struggle to keep the rubber on the road when Land Cruisers zipped by us, spraying us with clouds of dust and small rocks and leaving us wobbling precariously in their unthinking wake.

The occupants of most of the vehicles turned their heads as they passed us, craning to get a better look at the two idiots on motorcycles. Almost every Chinese tourist took a photograph of us, while most of the Western tourists raised their hands in restrained but friendly greeting. We experienced similar cultural differences in people's reactions throughout the trip: some people stopped us and asked a thousand questions; some rushed up to us excitedly and included us in their photographs before bustling away again, giggling like children; and others winked at us and nodded almost imperceptibly, as if to say, 'You're living my dream.'

At one point on our journey that day, we stopped near a small shack from which a piece of string was stretched across the road and tied to a pole on the other side. A man came to the door of what was really little more than a hut and asked to see our Mount Everest Base Camp National Park tickets. When we handed them to him, he examined them carefully, loosened the piece of string so that it dropped to the ground, and then waved us on our way, along a track that curled around the side of a mountain. And then, suddenly, there in front of us was Everest.

'We made it! We made it, bro!' Colin shouted into his Bluetooth headset. I could feel tears pricking my eyes. We *had* made it, together. My sense of having accomplished something important was overwhelming.

I'd been to Everest before, when I hiked around China on my own in 2001. It was mid-November and very cold and I'd had to camp several times on my way; getting there had been a real struggle. This time, I'd ridden to Everest with my brother on a motorcycle, and somehow it was a completely different experience. On my previous visit, I don't remember the mountain looking as dramatic and majestic as it did at that moment, or later, after we'd traveled the last few kilometers on the tourist bus and Colin and I sat on a rock watching the sun set behind the highest mountain peak in the world. Base Camp is 5200 meters above sea level, and although it must have been freezing up there, I didn't even notice the temperature.

A week earlier, we'd been on our way to Everest when we'd had to take a detour to Lhasa to get my bike fixed and hadn't known if we were going to be able to continue with our trip. We'd had to deal with frustrations, anxieties, and added costs, and then we'd had to backtrack more than 600 km. It had all been worthwhile, because it had led to the moment when I stood in the shadow of Mount Everest with my brother beside me. I was really proud to have made it there, despite everything, and I don't think there are words that can adequately describe the enormous sense of achievement I felt.

Colin and I have talked about that day many times since then, and we agree that it was the most exciting and challenging day we'd spent on the bikes, as well as the most memorable experience of our lives. It took us 9 hours to cover 75 km of incredibly difficult off-roading at an altitude of between 4500 and 5200 meters above sea level. It's a road we'll never forget.

Day 45 (*27 September 2010*)

I get down when we're not moving; it feels like we're not accomplishing anything. So being on the road again lifted my spirits. You really appreciate riding when you've had a few days off.

We tested Ryan's bike repeatedly while we were riding this morning; it was such a relief that it kept going, and we arrived early in Shigatse and had a nice dinner. What we're really focused on now is Everest Base Camp the day after tomorrow: it's one of the things I've been looking forward to most on this trip.

Day 46 (*28 September 2010*)

I had my first sight of Everest today: it was totally amazing!

When we arrived at the small farming village where we're staying tonight, some kids ran up to us and started

---

poking our pockets, saying 'Hello. Money.' They were really funny, friendly little kids, so we did what any caring adult would do, and, with complete disregard for their dental health, gave them some of the lollipops Chad has brought with him to help him quit smoking.

We talked to some of the women who were working in the fields and they told us that they earn 20 RMB a day when they're just rolling hay, like they were doing today, and 30 RMB during the harvest. That's about $3 and $4.5 respectively, which, despite probably being more than I thought they'd earn, isn't very much.

We're just 80 km from Everest Base Camp. We should do that in about 4 or 5 hours tomorrow. Apparently, we won't be able to ride our bikes right up to the camp – you have to hop on a tourist bus for the last couple of kilometers, which is disappointing, although it shouldn't have been a surprise in the light of past experience here. However we get there, I just can't wait!

Day 47 (29 September 2010)
Today was the day I've looked forward to throughout this entire trip – and it more than lived up to my expectations.

The ride to Everest Base Camp was stunning. There was no road, just a track, which only exists at all because other people have driven along it. Apart from a few other tourists in cars, all we saw were yak, sheep, and goats. And now here I am, at Base Camp, with Mount Everest right behind me. How fucking cool is that!

Base Camp isn't quite what I was expecting: I thought Everest would tower above it like some sort of massive monolithic beacon. But because the camp itself is at 5200 meters above sea level, the mountain doesn't look *that* big from here. It is an incredible view though: the valley opens up ahead of you and all you can see is Everest. It's surrounded by other high peaks – I hadn't realized there were so many almost-as-high mountains around it – but you can't see them from Base Camp. It's a phenomenal, indescribable sight. I'd like to come back here one day and try to climb it.

Today has been a day I will never, ever forget.

Chapter 20

Eastern Tibet is closed to foreigners

After watching the sun rise over Everest the next morning, we left Base Camp and had a tough 80-km ride on bad roads, through a valley, and then up 20 km of switch-backs to a high pass where the sound of the wind was almost deafening as it whipped hundreds of prayer flags into a frenzy of motion.

At 6.30 that evening, about 330 km later, we were rolling along Highway G318 back into Shigatse when I recognized my shadow ahead of me for the first time: we were heading east, to Shanghai, and from that point onwards, I'd be following my shadow every afternoon on roads that would take me closer to my family. I was having a great time, but the thought of going home and picking up my regular life again made my heart beat just a little bit faster.

We continued to backtrack from Shigatse to Lhasa the next day, which turned out to be an incredibly disappointing one, mainly because we were refused permits to enter Eastern Tibet and travel to Yunnan Province along Highway G318. The reason we were given was that, following recent civil disturbances, the whole area had been closed to foreigners. There are often protests against the Chinese government in Eastern Tibet, and as it was October 1st, which is National Day and a holiday in China, suspicion was at an even higher level and security was tighter than normal, which meant that whereas Chinese people were still allowed to use the road, foreigners were not.

We'd encountered checkpoints almost every 200 km throughout our journey, and with each passing day I'd become increasingly aware of how militarized China really is. Now it looked as though we'd traveled 13,000 km just to be told, 'You can't go that way. You'll have to backtrack 2000 km north, and then another 3000 km south again.' It was a huge disappointment, which left me feeling angry and frustrated, and by the end of the day I'd completely lost my sense of humor.

As a foreigner in China, you're discriminated against – sometimes favorably, for example because you have the opportunity to get better, higher-paid jobs than those that are open to most Chinese nationals, particularly in the big cities. The flip side of that coin is that, in remote country regions you're viewed, by the military at least, as a potential criminal and are banned from the many 'sensitive areas', even if all you want to do is pass through them.

Without the necessary permits to travel by road through Eastern Tibet, we had two options.

The first option was to go anyway and drive through the checkpoints at night. The problem was that the sun sets at about 8 p.m. in Tibet and by 9 p.m. the temperature is well below zero: sneaking through checkpoints on our motorcycles in sub-zero conditions in the pitch dark didn't hold any appeal. More importantly, we discovered that the checkpoints on that particular road are manned by the military, not the police, and we knew that whereas policemen *might* be persuaded to let us pass, soldiers would not. It would be one thing if Colin, Chad, and I got caught – another of the upsides of being a foreigner in China is that it's likely to provide you with a get-out-of-jail-free card in that sort of situation. But it would have meant something quite different for our amazing guide, Kalsang, who is Tibetan.

That left us with the second of our two options: to put our bikes on a truck that would take them through Eastern Tibet, while we had a rest day in Lhasa and then flew to our next destination – Zhondian in Yunnan Province – in time to meet the truck, collect our motorcycles, and continue our journey by road.

It wasn't the Middle Kingdom Ride as we'd planned it: it meant missing 1200 km of riding through the Three Rivers Region, where mountain ranges divide the Salween, Mekong, and Yangtze rivers in what's probably one of the most beautiful parts of Tibet. I'd been looking forward to showing the extraordinary landscapes to my brother. But we both knew that no amount of reasoned argument was going to change the minds of the people responsible for making the decision to deny us travel permits. It was one of many occasions on our journey when we simply had to accept that rules were rules. It was incredibly disappointing.

In Lhasa the next day, we booked our flights to Zhondian and then put our motorcycles on a truck that would make the journey we should have been making through Eastern Tibet. The region had been closed to foreigners for at least a month prior to our leaving Shanghai, and although I'd tried to get the necessary travel permits, they hadn't come through before we left, so I'd been relying on it being opened again by the time we reached Lhasa. There was no way of knowing when the situation would change – the restrictions might be lifted the next day or they might remain in place for weeks – and we couldn't wait in Lhasa forever.

On the morning of day 51 of our journey, we flew 1200 km from Lhasa in Tibet to Zhongdian (which was recently renamed Shangri-La) in Yunnan Province, where we would wait for our bikes to arrive on the truck, which we hoped would be within a couple of days. I felt gutted.

Tibet is beautiful: I love the friendly, smiling people and I love the culture. When I'd had time to think about it, however, I decided I probably wouldn't be rushing back there. I've never been very keen on authority, or on being told what to do and when to do it – part of the appeal of working as a freelance photographer is that I'm able, quite literally, to call my own shots – and in Tibet I felt smothered by bureaucracy.

I was tired of being stopped at checkpoints, having to answer questions about the bikes, and trying not to show any sign of irritation when some potentially angry 18-year-old with an AK47 examined my passport and travel permit and then searched through my pannier bags, making me feel like a fugitive with something to hide. In some towns in Tibet, we were stopped, questioned, and searched at military *and* police checkpoints, and I resented each pointless, frustrating waste of up to an hour of my life.

To me, riding a motorcycle is all about being free: it's just you, the bike, and the open road – and that's a great feeling. As a motorcycle tourist and adventure rider in Tibet, it felt as if that sense of freedom was being stamped on and crushed. I'd really looked forward to traveling through Tibet with my brother, and I never thought I'd be glad to be back in eastern China. But at least in China proper you aren't confronting authority every day and you don't have so many encounters with the military. In some ways, Tibet *was* the highlight of the journey, as I'd expected it to be, if only because of its extraordinary beauty.

We were 5000 km from Shanghai – the same distance away from it that we'd been 5 days earlier when we'd stopped beside the marker on Highway G318. Colin and I were tired and my spirits were low, although not low enough to consider quitting the trip and flying home. As we entered the fourth and final stage of our journey – the home stretch – I wondered what new challenges lay ahead for us.

Day 49 *(1 October 2010)*

There's been a change of plan. We've been off our bikes more than we've been on them for the last couple of weeks, and it isn't over yet. Eastern Tibet is still closed to foreigners and security in the area has been tightened – because of the October holiday – rather than relaxed, as we'd hoped it would be. It's *so* frustrating.

Our guide found a monk who said he'd drive us through the checkpoints at night! Ryan and I weighed the risks and possible outcomes involved and decided that it doesn't make sense to risk our guide and driver being reprimanded or punished. We thought about taking the train north with the bikes and then heading back south again. But, like all the other options we considered, that would take too much time, and therefore too much money. We're paying the guides and drivers a daily rate, so extending the trip by at least another 12 days, which is what it would mean, isn't a viable option.

The prospect of flying to Shangri-La (Zhongdian) and missing out on seeing Eastern Tibet is really disappointing. What's even worse is looking over your shoulder all the time and wondering if you're doing something wrong. It's the first time in my life I've been controlled by a government – or, at least, that I've been aware of it! It makes me really angry. There must be better ways of doing things.

Day 50 (2 October 2010)

Last night, we tried, without success, to find a truck driver who'd be willing and able to take the bikes through Eastern Tibet – every day they aren't moving is a lost day of riding and an added expense. We found a driver quite quickly this morning, and as soon as we'd loaded the bikes onto his truck, we bought planes tickets for a flight to Shangri-La tomorrow, and I started to feel better about things.

It was a big decision, and I think we made the right one. It's frustrating, but it's time to move on and forget about it: dwelling on something we can't alter will only affect our enjoyment going forward. So we spent today blogging and updating the Middle Kingdom Ride website. Then I got a massage and we chatted to some really nice ex-pat foreigners we met at the hotel. It was fun talking to people and sharing our stories.

Tomorrow, when we fly to Shangri-La, it will be the first time in weeks when we'll feel that we're in China proper.

Day 51 (3 October 2010)

This morning, we were driven to the airport by a monk! The flight took 1½ hours and was a good local Chinese flight experience.

We've spent 3 weeks in Tibet, which is the longest we've been in any region. It was both the most rewarding and the most difficult part of our trip, and included some serious highs and lows. Despite everything that went wrong while we were there, I'm sad to have left. It was the people who made it such a good experience for me. I've met a few individual Buddhists before, but I'd never really known what they believed in, and I was really impressed by the way Buddhists *live* their beliefs by being generous, kind, friendly, honest, and helpful. I'm sad not to have seen more of Tibet and the Tibetans, particularly because the reality is that I'll probably never go back there.

On the upside, the next part of our journey is exciting too. We're back in China proper, not far from the border with Burma, and the landscape has changed completely. Because it rains a lot, everything is green, and the mountains are more like rolling hills covered in thick vegetation.

We'll ride hard for the next couple of weeks and then this epic journey will be over. I'm ready for that now: I'm tired and I'm missing my wife, and my Western life. So although I'm sorry to have left Tibet, I'm happy to be moving toward the finish line.

Chapter 21

The long road home

After two enforced rest days in Zhongdian, the bikes arrived at 4.30 in the morning of 6 October. We unloaded them off the truck, had another brief sleep, and then set off on the road again, heading south.

Getting out of the city was a nightmare of traffic and rain. We still had the off-road tires on our bikes, which aren't designed to be used on wet tarmac, and when Colin took a corner with what I thought was a little too much speed, he slid right off the road. I was riding behind him, so I rounded the corner a few seconds later. What I heard over our biker-to-biker communication system made me feel sick with fear and apprehension, but I didn't see exactly what happened, because by the time I arrived on the scene, Colin and his bike had already hit the ground.

The motorcycle had slid one way, ending up in a ditch, and Colin had slid off the road in another direction and was lying beside a tree. There was a whole jumble of thoughts racing through my mind. Then I heard Colin's voice yelling, 'It's okay; I'm okay,' and the fear subsided just enough to enable me to breathe again. When I got off my bike and ran over to him, it was clear that he was shaken. Miraculously though, apart from some quite severe bruising, he seemed relatively unscathed – particularly considering what *could* have happened to him.

The parts of the plastic frame of his bike that weren't actually shattered were cracked, and the steering column was bent. It wasn't damage we could fix at the side of the road, but we did manage to straighten the steering enough to enable him to carry on.

Although I hated taking the role of big brother, as Colin mounted his bike again, I couldn't help saying, in a tone I hoped sounded casual, 'Perhaps it would be a good idea to take the corners a bit slower in the wet.' I guess it didn't even need to be said.

We rode on, dodging the trucks whose tires were sending out a thick spray of oily water as they sped along the highway, and I tried not to think about what we might have been doing at that moment if, for example, there'd been a car coming the other way on the wrong side of the road, which is a very common event in China. It was at times like that when the reality of what we were doing and the risks we were taking really hit home. You don't have any protection when you're riding a motorcycle: there's no steel chassis or sheet metal to help shield you on impact, and two wheels are a good deal less stable than four. If you fall, you fall. It doesn't matter why or whose fault it is; what happens next is in the lap of the gods and you can really hurt yourself, or worse.

I did think that Colin sometimes rode a bit too fast – although I accept that that's an impression that may have had more to do with my own wish to protect him than with reality. Even so, as we continued along the highway that morning, the big-brother voice in my head muttered darkly, 'He's going to have to pull it together over the next few days if he's going to get home safely.'

The trip had initially been my idea, and it had been *my* knowledge of China that had informed the route we were taking. So I felt responsible. I didn't want my little brother getting hurt *at all*, but I really, really didn't want him to get hurt on my watch, and I felt that, on that day, I hadn't protected him as I should have done: it was luck that had saved him from serious injury. I didn't know how to process what had happened; it almost made me want to stop the trip and put our bikes and ourselves on a train to Shanghai.

Quite apart from my own concerns, I felt that it was important for us to have a good day the next day, so that Colin could put the crash behind him and get his confidence back, and, thankfully, things did go more smoothly. In the morning, we removed the off-road tires, replaced them with street tires, and did oil changes on both bikes. The new tires made a huge difference, and despite not setting off until 1 p.m., we managed to do about 350 km that day.

When we left Dali, the temperature was about 10° Celsius and it was raining. I thought it would get warmer as the day progressed; in fact, it did just the opposite: for the next 6 hours, the temperature fell steadily, the rain never let up, and the wind howled. By the time we reached Kunming, we were soaking wet and miserably cold, but at least we'd been moving and felt that we were getting somewhere.

That night, although I was happy with the way the day had gone, I was pessimistic about how hard the next 10 to 14 days were going to be. I wasn't tired of the trip; I was mentally and physically exhausted by the intense weather conditions. A pattern seemed to have developed so that I slept more heavily every night, took longer to wake up every morning, and was so tired again at the end of the day that I struggled to stay awake long enough to have something to eat before crashing out. On the plus side, I *did* still feel upbeat and optimistic in the mornings. We'd never thought the journey was going to be easy, but with my increasing tiredness came an increasing concern about our ability to return safely to Shanghai. If something were to happen to one of us, no part of what we'd done would have been worth doing.

The next day was the third consecutive day when we rode through torrential rain. We did 522 km from Kunming to the city of Guiyang in temperatures that didn't rise above 12° Celsius. At least the roads were good, and as they wound their way up the mountains, beside rice paddies, through tunnels, and across the vast expanses of bridges, the views were spectacular. Unfortunately, because of the relentless rain, we got very little film footage. One thing Chad *did* manage to immortalize on video, however, was the moment when we'd stopped for a drink of water and Colin attempted to warm his frozen bits by standing close to the muffler on his bike!

The following day, it rained again, although, thankfully, it was warm. We took the expressway out of Guiyang and then rode the rest of the way to Rongjiang, in Guizhou Province, on secondary roads. Despite the heavy truck traffic, we zipped along Highway S308, past more rice terraces and little villages that seemed to be clinging to the sides of the mountains. In the last 4 days, we'd traveled 1500 km in rain and it was becoming clear that we were directly underneath a huge rain cloud that was moving with us from west to east. It might have been tempting to stay put and wait for the cloud to pass, if it hadn't been for the very realistic possibility that it might continue to rain for another week or more. There was nothing we could do except put our heads down and push on.

Again, I think Colin and I were helped by the fact that we'd done a lot of sports training at school and university. In sport, it doesn't matter how badly you've slept, how little you've had to eat, or how far you've traveled: when the game starts, you focus on what you've got to do and you do it to the very best of your ability. (It's an analogy that breaks down to some extent when you consider that, even allowing for timeouts and stoppages, a basketball game lasts for around 2½ hours, whereas we'd been on the road for 57 days!)

Day 54 *(6 October 2010)*

Today was interesting. The bikes arrived at 4.30 this morning – which seems to be the standard bike-arrival time in China. After some more sleep, we set off and everything was going pretty well – the landscape was more like Switzerland or British Columbia than anything I'd imagined in China – and then it started to rain.

The rain wasn't heavy, but the mud on the road made it slippery, and we were still using our off-road tires, which don't have very good grip on tarmac. I don't know how fast I was going when I rounded the corner; it didn't seem to be very fast. When I tried to steer, the rear tire didn't respond and just kept going straight. I tapped the brakes, and got nothing. Then I tried to engine brake, and still I got nothing. It was at that moment that I knew I was going to go off the road, and all I could do was buckle down and head for a gap in the trees and bushes.

Ryan said I was probably going a bit too fast for the road conditions when I came round the corner. He may have been right, but I'd like to say in my defense that there were at least two smashed car windshields in the ditch near where I crashed. On second thoughts, perhaps that isn't so much a good defense as an indication that it was a dangerous corner and I wasn't the first person to have taken it too fast!

Whatever the reason for what happened, it was the scariest fall of my life. Despite the fact that I sprained my thumb and bruised my right leg pretty badly, I know I was lucky, and that things could have turned out a lot worse.

Even after the crash, I still enjoyed the ride, although thinking about all the 'what ifs' made me realize I've got to be more careful. We saw *nine* other accidents today. The road was winding, wet, and greasy. (Okay, so maybe I *should* have been going a little slower when I hit that corner.) The bike got quite badly broken and I rode about 230 km after my fall with a skewed front wheel, bent handlebars, and some liberally applied duck tape. It was fine – or, at least, it was good enough to get us to our next stop.

We arrived in Dali at about 9 p.m., in the dark, which was really dangerous. Fortunately, we got there safely, maybe thanks to the white scarves Kalsang gave Ryan and me before he flew back to Tibet this morning – apparently, Tibetan people give them to each other as a talisman for 'safety on long journeys'.

Despite the fact that it was a tough day, it felt good to be back on the road.

Day 55 (7 October 2010)
We found a mechanic in Dali who had a machine for taking tires off rims. Everyone helped out and they did a good job, so we got a lot done in a short period of time. We've got a great team.

Your confidence is shattered after a crash, and today helped to boost mine again. Even so, I spent most of the day second-guessing myself, because I thought that even if I *did* go into the corner too fast yesterday, I should have been able to control it.

If you ask bikers what they hate most, the majority will probably tell you 'rain' or 'cold' – and the two together are just shit. Well, it rained all fucking day and it was really cold. Ryan says that this part of the country is lovely; I'll have to take his word for it, because the clouds were so low we couldn't see anything. At the end of the day, I poured a good inch of water out of my boots, and my heels were so numb they'd turned white.

The upside is that days like today make you believe that you can do anything. Ryan and I are both very competitive, and I feel proud when I know I've really pushed myself. We snuck onto the expressway, which I don't like doing, but it was good to get 350 km under our belts. For me, the day was a much-needed confidence booster.

Day 56 (8 October 2010)
The fact that I'm still happy after riding more than 500 km in the cold and rain must say something – I'm not sure whether it's something about resilience, cussed determination not to be beaten, a previously unsuspected tendency toward masochism, or the pure pleasure of riding a motorcycle through some of what must be the most gorgeous scenery in China. The

landscape we rode through today was what I imagine Vietnam or Cambodia to be like.

The road was great too. It was possibly the most impressive example of road building I've ever seen in my life. Instead of winding its way around the mountains via a series of switch-backs, it cut straight through them – bridge, tunnel, bridge, tunnel ... Sometimes it was like riding through the clouds. The mountains are a lush green color, and there are lots of tiny villages that seem to be suspended in mid-air. It was a wonderful ride – apart from the weather.

My brother recently won an award for a picture he'd taken of an amazing bridge on the road we were on today, and it was the first time he'd ridden across it since the construction work had been completed. He loves this country so much and he's so passionate about sharing it with other people that I felt quite emotional riding over that bridge with him – and it *is* extraordinary, both as a triumph of engineering and as a thing of beauty, standing in the middle of nowhere, hundreds of feet above the floor of the valley.

Now, I'm off to try to warm up in the hot tub, which, rumor has it, can be found somewhere in the hotel we're staying in tonight.

Day 57 (9 October 2010)
It fucking rained again today! I'm *so* tired of being wet. When all your shit's soaking, you don't even want to

stop for lunch. Will the rain ever end? It's beginning to look like the answer's no.

At least it's warm now, and, despite spending the last 4 days riding in the rain, I'm still enjoying the scenery – that really says something. Today, we rode through the most sensational landscape I've ever seen in my entire life – rice terraces and little wooden houses that looked as though they were so precariously balanced on the sides of cliffs that a puff of wind would blow them off. It was like riding through Avatar or some other sci-fi world, or perhaps the place where ninjas are born! I had no idea that landscape like that existed in China: I've never even seen pictures of it.

Chapter 22

The Li River

By the time we reached the town of Guilin in Guangxi Province, we were just 2400 km from home. We did 336 km that day, along switch-backs through gorgeous scenery, and it was the first day since leaving Zhongdian 5 days earlier when we didn't get rained on. It was also the first day when we'd really been able to look around us as we were riding, rather than having to concentrate on avoiding potholes and puddles on the road and on not braking so hard that the bikes aquaplaned out of control. What we *did* have to watch out for was the road construction, and the water buffalo that sometimes wandered out in front of us.

I'd had an email a few days earlier from someone who asked what the toughest aspect of the trip had been so far: my answer was, unequivocally, the weather – the rain, hail, snow, wind, and sandstorms, the incredible heat at the start of the journey, and the almost unbearable cold at the Pakistan border. That day, however, when we were on the way from Rongjiang to Guilin, the rain stopped and everything else paled into insignificance compared to the pleasure of riding through a landscape of glorious colors and distinctive karst formations. By the end of the day, my notebook was full of the names of places I want to revisit with my camera.

Each day was like the swing of a pendulum and I was struggling to find the motivation to keep moving. I still felt that the journey we were on was important and exhilarating – I knew that it was a once-in-a-lifetime trip that would change me and my brother forever. But I'd got to the point of waking up in the mornings and having to dig deep to find any real enthusiasm for whatever lay ahead that day.

Day 59 was a rest day, and we woke up early and drove down to the Li River, which is one of the most scenically impressive regions in China. We rented an eight-seat boat with a driver and as we puttered down the river between steep karst formations covered in lush, subtropical vegetation and rice terraces, we began to relax and enjoy the experience of being passengers for a while. It was like being inside a picture painted from someone's imagination to depict the most beautiful place in the world.

After 4 hours, the driver of the boat pulled up alongside the riverbank in what appeared to be the middle of nowhere, nodded his head in the direction of nothing that we could see, and said 'Yangshou is that way.'

'Great. Well, can you drop us in the town?' I asked.

He shrugged as he answered, 'No. I have to leave you here.' And as soon as we'd stepped out of the boat, he reversed away from the riverbank and headed back in the direction from which we'd just come.

Fortunately – although not, of course, coincidentally – there was a rank of motorcycle taxis on the road above the riverbank. That's how things work in the designated tourist spots in China: everyone does their bit and gets their chance to make some money out of the tourists, and then they pass you on to someone else. And it was fun riding on the back of a motorcycle taxi for the 5 minutes it took to get into town.

Yangshou is the largest hippie backpacker hangout in the whole of China. The town is full of people who've gone there on vacation and are still there 2 years later, drinking cheap alcohol and smoking the marijuana that grows so abundantly in the surrounding mountains. I guess life there is uncomplicated, and if you need to earn a living, you can probably find work as an English teacher in one of the many language schools.

Almost as soon as we hit town, we were accosted by four Chinese girls who were studying English and who'd been sent out onto the streets by their teacher to talk to English-speaking foreigners. After a lot of giggling and some language practice, the girls asked us to sign their 'foreigner books', and then Chad and I caught up with Colin, who was standing by a market stall piled high with the pirated DVDs that make China so unpopular with the film industry in the West.

When we left Yangshou, we picked up the car in Guilin and drove along a route that took in a couple of the small villages beside the river, including one in which a large sign above a shop announced it to be 'The S & M Hairdresser'.

Later that afternoon, when we parked the car and a parking attendant tried to charge me double the clearly advertised cost of 5 RMB, I did something I'd never normally have done and became involved in a verbal altercation with him. When I asked him for a receipt for the 10 RMB he was insisting I had to pay, he refused to give me one, and I was incensed – perhaps partly because I was tired and suffering the effects of having been on the road too long. We were arguing over 5 RMB – that's less than US$1 (50p). But it was the principle that mattered, and the fact that all the frustrations of the last couple of weeks were simmering away just below the surface, ready to boil over at the slightest provocation.

It was a good thing we'd soon be home.

Day 58 *(10 October 2010)*
I was dry today for the first time in 5 days. It would be good to be able to say that the sun came out and it was glorious weather, but although the temperature did reach 25° Celsius, it drizzled a few times – which is what passes for a nice day at the moment! At least we could see the scenery, and our clothes didn't stick to us like a cold, moist poultice.

There's always a yang to every yin, however, and today's downside was the fact that the chains on both our bikes started to make a rather worrying noise. We couldn't work out what was causing it, so we stopped every hour or so and applied chain lube, which dealt with the noise, even if it was doing nothing to address the underlying problem.

Guilin seems like a nice city; it's touristy, but modern and quite switched on, and we're staying in a good hotel.

Day 59 (11 October 2010)

Today was a really good day. The boat trip was amazing: I felt like I was on a hunt for Godzilla! You quickly run out of adjectives in China: 'amazing', 'beautiful', 'incredible' all start to sound clichéd and over-used. The landscape we saw today was all of those things and more.

I was thinking today about tourism in China and how it's controlled here, from a business perspective, in terms of tourist sites and the building of airports, roads, and places where people can set up shops. I've seen a lot of lovely places on this trip and it's interesting to speculate on why particular ones are chosen as designated tourist sites. It's all part of the ethos in China, I suppose: they want to attract tourists, but only to the parts they want them to see. There's no free travel here; it's all structured: you're taken on a tour bus to the place where you're allowed to get off, then you get on the bus again and are taken somewhere else. Coming from a country where you can explore wherever you want, I find that interesting.

We did go off the beaten track for a while today, taking a remote road down to the river. When we got back onto a paved road, we parked at an 'official' spot and Ryan had an argument with a parking attendant. I really do get that it's frustrating for my brother when people treat him like a tourist and try to overcharge him, because he's lived here for 10 years. That's why, throughout this trip, we've sent our guides to do the negotiating whenever money has needed to be paid. We only appear once a price has been agreed; otherwise, we'd be constantly ripped off.

When we were on the boat, I called home. My wife is at my dad's house in the US and they were having dinner to celebrate Canadian Thanksgiving.

We've got about a week more of riding to do before we reach Shanghai. Now that our rest day is over, it's started to rain again!

Chapter 23

The final hurdle

On the day we left Guilin, we did 576 km. It was almost like rewinding parts of our journey, because we drove through rain, sunshine, around road construction, up mountains, down mountains, past farming villages, on good roads, and on bad roads. We were in the Pearl River delta, heading east to the town of Shaoguan, in Guangdong Province. There are a lot of factories in that area and the roads are congested, so we'd opted to travel on secondary roads to avoid the heavy traffic. It was frustrating not to be able to drive fast, and the next day we decided to take expressways the rest of the way home to Shanghai.

The day we left Guilin was long and intense, although, in retrospect, its pace was almost leisurely compared to the next day, when we did an incredible 864 km in a little over 9 hours. The weather was sunny and the fact that we were riding on the expressway meant that we were bypassing all the slow-moving trucks and cars on the secondary roads.

There's a misconception that driving fast on a motorcycle on an expressway is dangerous; in reality, it was probably the safest driving we'd done throughout the entire trip. Everyone's going in the same direction; you've got maybe 3 km of visibility; there are no potholes on the road (the road surface was perfectly paved); and there are no cows or water buffalo waiting to wander out in front of you. On a dry road, a motorcycle can stop in half the distance required by a car – as long as you brake properly: slam on your back brake and you'll skid; hit the front brake too hard and you'll go over the handlebars.

We took a ferry for the last part of our journey that day, and stayed the night in Xiamen, which is a large, fast-paced city in Fujian Province, opposite Taiwan. The next day, we woke up late and traveled about 280 km north up the coast to Fuzhou. The last 3 days had been exhausting. In the last 62, we'd traveled 17,000 km, and now we were on the home stretch; our heads were down and our minds were focused on getting back to Shanghai. It was time to put an end to the trip. All we had to do now was make sure it ended safely.

The major downside of traveling on expressways was that it involved playing cat and mouse with the police, which was something neither Colin nor I liked doing. But it was the only way we could make good progress, and on the occasions when the police *did* catch us, they didn't really know what to do about us, so they let us go. If we set out to do 300 km on a secondary road, we'd have no idea how long it was going to take us, except that it could be anything up to 8 hours; whereas on an expressway we knew it would take about 3. That was a big difference, particularly at that stage of our journey, and as we *really* wanted to get home, we'd probably have taken almost any risk that didn't involve jeopardizing our physical safety.

While we were in Fuzhou, we visited the factory where Andreas – a long-time friend of mine who's an avid motorcyclist and the guy who pulled out all the stops to get a clutch for us when we were stuck in Lhasa – is a director. Andreas couldn't be there that day, so two great co-workers of his, Andreas Quade and Andrew Kay, showed us around.

The company, which is called *framas*, makes the plastic pieces that go on the bottom of sports shoes – mostly rugby, soccer, golf, and running shoes. That probably doesn't sound too interesting, except perhaps to a sports fanatic, whereas it's actually a fascinating process to watch. And, of course, you can't go to China without visiting a factory.

We watched people dyeing pellets of plastic, pressing them into molds, trimming them to the shape of the bottom of a shoe, and then embedding them with spikes. They were also making the little plastic nubs that go on the bottom of the spikes on rugby and soccer boots – each one of which is of a size and shape specific to its particular location – as well as the plastic stripes for the Adidas logo, and in the same factory they were recycling all the waste material and making it into little bags.

I visit a lot of factories during the course of my work, and I learn something new every single time, but Colin had never been to any sort of factory anywhere before, and he found the processes and talking to some of the people who were working there really interesting.

We left Fuzhou after lunch and rode about 350 km up the coast, arriving at our next stop – the town of Wenzhou – at 3 o'clock in the afternoon. The hotel we'd booked in Wenzhou was a good one, judging by all the Bentleys, Aston Martins, and Porsches that were in the car park when we pulled in. We had stuff to unpack from our bikes, so we rode up to the front of the hotel, and immediately a bellboy launched himself out of the door and tried to stop us.

I was tired, and I was fed up of having to explain to people that they weren't 150-cc scooters, they were 800-cc motorcycles, which cost as much as some of the cars parked nearby. That's probably why I lost it – first with the bellboy and then with the hotel manager, who apologized profusely and upgraded our rooms.

We were approaching the end of our journey – we were so close to Shanghai I could almost smell it. The prospect of a journey's end can be sad or even depressing, but what was really good about it was that we were going to get our lives back. I'd been on an extraordinary adventure with my brother, and I knew I'd need time to reflect on everything we'd seen and experienced before the reality of what we'd actually accomplished sank in. More immediately, the thought of being in Shanghai again with my wife gave me goose bumps; I'd really missed her.

No one wants to be the guy who goes on an amazing trip and complains all the time, but I didn't know it was going to be so hard! It had been much, much more difficult than I'd imagined. In fact, that isn't really a complaint, because the difficulties made it all the more rewarding. I was proud of what Colin and I had achieved: we'd dedicated 2 months of our lives – 2 months that we'd taken away from our families – to completing the challenge we'd set ourselves, and we were about to become the first people ever to have circumnavigated China by motorcycle.

The next morning, Colin and I woke up feeling good. We'd been riding on the expressways consequence-free, and we decided to do it again that day. Instead of taking a ticket at the toll booths, we rode around the barriers. Sometimes, the toll operators yelled at us, and one or two even left their booths and stepped in front of our motorcycles or, more rarely, made a grab for one of us. None of them ever chased us though, or even radioed ahead to warn the people at the next toll that we were on our way. We'd passed police in cars while riding on expressways and even they had done nothing to stop us. I guess once you're on the road it isn't their problem, so they leave it to the guys at the tollgates to sort it out.

It certainly wasn't a relaxing way to travel; on the other hand, a few minutes of discomfort was a small price to pay for being able to speed toward home at 120 kph instead of maybe half that. Even in the rain, we could do up to 80 kph on the expressways, and it was much safer than using the back roads: the more you have to brake, accelerate, and gear-shift – which you're doing constantly when you're driving amongst cars and trucks on minor roads – the more likely you are to have a fall.

On this particular day, we'd been riding for about 20 minutes since dodging around the barrier at the tollgate when a police officer, who'd been standing at the side of the road, jumped out into the first lane of the highway and tried to flag us down. It was too dangerous for us even to attempt to stop and, shocked by the insanity of what the police officer was doing and by the realization of how close he'd come to causing a terrible accident and a massive pile-up of fast-moving trucks and cars, we blew past him. It was easily one of the most hazardous moments of our journey and it left Colin and me feeling deeply shaken – and then I began to worry about the possibility of having to face similar encounters with the police on the road ahead.

When we stopped for gas, it was clear that Colin was as anxious as I was. But there didn't seem to be any alternative other than to rejoin the expressway, which was what we were about to do when Colin noticed a man on a bicycle go through a small gap at the back of the gas station. We followed the cyclist, and ended up in a village, which led us onto a secondary road that ran almost parallel to the expressway. We'll never know whether we avoided a roadblock and a confrontation with the police, or whether they'd simply shrugged their shoulders and forgotten about us.

There'd been so many other things to think about that we hadn't really worked out exactly what route we were going to take into Shanghai. The direct route involved going over a bridge, which I knew we wouldn't be allowed to do on motorcycles: whereas the tolls on expressways are manned by civilian toll-booth operators, bridges are military, and no one in their right mind would try to bust through a military tollgate. What that meant was that, instead of being able to cut across the bay, we'd have to go all the way around it to the city of Hangzhou and then head north to Shanghai. It would add about 700 km to our journey home, which, when we saw the volume of traffic on the roads, we realized would mean at least another 2 days of traveling.

On the night of day 64, we stayed at a hotel on the tiny, pretty island of Putoshan, off the coast of Zhejiang Province, in the East China Sea, and tried to plan a different route home: there had to be some way of bypassing the bridge that didn't involve such a long detour.

The next morning, we woke up at 5 o'clock, drove to the dock, and pulled in behind the line of vehicles that were already waiting to board a ferry that would take them to the container shipping terminal at the off-shore port of Yangshan.

We'd only been in line for a few minutes when a security guard told us, 'No motorcycles allowed on the ferry.'

'We got here on a ferry,' I told him. 'Our motorcycles were allowed on that ferry. Why wouldn't they be allowed on this one?'

'Because of the bridge,' the guard said firmly. 'No motorcycles on the bridge, so no motorcycles on the ferry.'

My home and my family, who I hadn't seen for 65 days, were just across the bay, and there was no way I was going to accept having to drive another 700 km to get there. A few minutes later, when yelling like an exhausted toddler hadn't persuaded the security guard to change his mind, a blue truck pulled into line behind us – empty. After a brief negotiation with the driver, we employed our, by now well-practiced, skill of lifting the motorcycles onto the back of a truck, and then climbed up beside them.

I would have loved to have been able to ride my motorcycle across the 32.5-km Donghai Bridge, which connects Yangshan with mainland Shanghai and is one of the longest sea bridges in the world. But when the ferry stopped, we stayed with our bikes on the truck, cursing officials and officialdom and everyone who has ever insisted on enforcing a rule that doesn't make any sense.

Once we were off the ferry and over the bridge, we took the bikes off the truck and rode the last few kilometers into Shanghai, past the 2010 Expo site on the banks of the Huanpu River, and along the elevated highway to my home. When we'd set out 65 days earlier, we hadn't known when we'd be back, so there was no fanfare or party to welcome us. In those 65 days, we'd traveled 17,493 kilometers (10,846 miles) to become the first people to circumnavigate China on motorcycles, and we'd made a film about our adventure. I can't put into words how that felt, and I can't express either what it felt like to see my wife and children again.

It hadn't been an incredibly long motorcycle journey, compared to the tens of thousands of kilometers some people do. But longer journeys that don't involve going over ground you've already covered encompass several different countries. China is the largest country in the world that it's possible to circumnavigate without backtracking, and it was for that – the longest continuous journey by motorcycle within a single country – that we were awarded a Guinness World Record in 2011 and included in the book *Guinness World Records 2012*.

In my video diary for Sunday, 17 October 2010, the long, thick, unkempt, and itchy beard that had been growing since we left Shanghai on 14 August has gone: the Middle Kingdom Ride was over.

Day 62 (14 October 2010)

I'm so excited to be almost home! When we left Guilin we were riding on twisty roads through what at one point seemed almost like dense rainforest. The landscape here changes so fast, and there are *so* many people in China. Before I came here, I thought it was a few big cities and vast expanses of countryside interspersed with little farming villages. So I was surprised when, in just one day, we drove through several towns that must have had populations of more than 1 million.

Yesterday, we did 864 km, which was the greatest distance we've traveled in a day on the whole trip. It

---

was all on expressways and we probably sneaked through at least ten tolls, which was sometimes difficult and a bit physical.

Today, when we were on the expressway again, we saw a burning bus. Luckily, everyone had got out of the bus before it caught fire, and no one was hurt. After the fire engine arrived and two lanes of the four-lane highway were opened again, a cop pulled us over and told us we couldn't ride on the expressway. Ryan asked him what he wanted us to do, in view of the fact that we were already on the road and the next exit was 30 km ahead – at Fuzhou, which was where we were going anyway. In the end, the cop said 'Okay,' and let us carry on.

Our support car had another flat tire yesterday: it seems that the spares they bought in Yunnan Province were fakes and they only lasted about 2000 km. Then, today, the guys were involved in an accident when our driver missed the turn off for our hotel and reversed into a Mercedes. They've had a terrible couple of days.

For me, the highlight of today was booking my ticket to Los Angeles to see my wife. It's great to have that to look forward to; the thought of it keeps me going when I'm really tired – which is pretty much all the time now.

Day 63 *(15 October 2010)*
We've met so many people on this journey who've been willing to help us just because they're good people and

they're interested in what we're trying to do. Andreas is one of those people: he used his own resources, money, and time to help us out and I can't thank him and the other people like him enough. I hope I'll step up to the mark like that when someone needs my help; I certainly plan to.

It was awesome to go to Andreas's factory today. Every day you use stuff and have no idea how it's made, how much effort it takes to make it, and how many people are involved in the process. I think what surprised me most about the factory in Fuzhou was how good the facilities and work conditions were, and the fact that people seemed to be happy to be working there. It completely contradicted the idea we have in the West of hot, noisy, cramped sweatshops. I'm sure there *are* places like that in China, but it was really encouraging to see that good places exist too.

After we'd visited the factory, we drove 350 km straight, without stopping or getting off our motorcycles. It was a record for me – and one that I'd be happy never to break! The main reason we opted not to stop was because we were on expressways and we didn't want to get pulled over by the police. At one toll, there was a group of police officers standing to one side when Ryan cruised through, and by the time I followed him, they were walking toward me. I just blew through too, with my heart racing because I didn't know what they'd do – nothing, was the answer, luckily.

Tomorrow should be the last day of having to sneak through tolls – the last day *ever* for me, I hope!

Day 64 *(16 October 2010)*

I lost my phone today, which really sucks. I suppose the only thing that's surprising about it is the fact that I managed to keep it for so long.

When we were in Tibet, I began to wonder if we'd be able to finish our trip on our bikes, and now, with just one more day to go, it looks as though we will. I've had an amazing time with my brother, and it feels really good to be on the verge of completing something that's been so challenging.

Day 65 *(17 October 2010)*

It's over! I can't believe it!

I had really mixed emotions driving into Shanghai today. Mostly what I feel is a sense of having accomplished something huge; it's the same sort of feeling I had when I graduated from university, when I sold my company, and when I got married. Those are the big events in my life I know I'll never forget, and today was the culmination of another one.

I fly out of China to LA in 48 hours. I'm *really* looking forward to seeing my wife.

I'm exhausted, I've run out of adrenalin, and I'm in shock: the fact that we did it still hasn't really sunk in. Within the last 65 days, I've had the best and the most intense experiences of my life, as well as the greatest swings of emotion: one day you're happy and the next day you're miserable, but both ends of the spectrum are on a scale that's completely different from the normal one of everyday life. And I'm going to miss Ryan and Chad.

I think I'm also going to miss not having new experiences every day. Despite all the obstacles and challenges we've had to deal with, there's something simple and straightforward about getting up every morning, getting on your bike, and riding; I'll miss that too. 'Real' life brings different issues that have to be dealt with.

Chapter 24

Lessons and legacies

Colin

I really had to dig deep on the trip, both mentally and physically. When I arrived in Shanghai a few days before we set out on the Middle Kingdom Ride, I found it hard to believe that we were really going; 65 days later, I found it even harder to believe it had actually taken place.

When we got back to Shanghai, Ryan's wife, Jasmine, asked me, 'So what do you think about China?' It was a question that would have taken another 65 days to answer fully. Perhaps my overriding sense was that I hadn't been traveling through a single country, but, rather, through China, Mongolia, Tibet, India, Central Asia, and then China again. I'd had no idea there was so much diversity – of people, religions, cultures, food, landscapes, climates ... The list is almost endless.

I don't think it's possible to travel anywhere for that length of time and not, at some stage, be frustrated almost to the point of losing it. As a white person in China, you're treated as someone of importance; as a motorcyclist, you're treated as a third-class citizen, at best. It was interesting – as well as sometimes infuriating – to experience those contrasts first-hand.

I know it will take some time for everything to sink in: when you've experienced something new every day for 65 days, you need time to reflect and to absorb the full impact of it all. If I had to choose the good, the bad, and the ugly right now, I'd say that a negative new experience for me was not being able to travel where I wanted when I wanted by whatever route I chose. I guess my biggest disappointment was not seeing Eastern Tibet. And the most positive thing about the trip was that my brother was able to show me what he loves about China, as well as what frustrates him: sharing both those things with him was very special.

It's easy to remember the mishaps and misfortunes; there were also many, many ways in which we were incredibly lucky, not least in terms of the caliber of the whole team of people who made it all possible for us. I met Chad just a couple of days before we set out and we got on really well. In fact, it was amazing how comfortable the three of us were in each other's company when we were traveling day after day in such close proximity.

During all those days with my brother, I spent only one night on my own – when we arrived at a hotel soaking wet and booked separate rooms so that we could dry out our stuff. I'll probably never spend so much time with him again. Ryan and I see some things very differently and we had disagreements, but never any fights. I think that's quite remarkable, and a testament to the strength and depth of our relationship, which I'm proud of.

What I'm very aware of, too, is how fortunate I was to be able to take the time off work and afford to do the trip at all. The decision to quit work and sell my house was one of the best decisions I've ever made. It's a cliché – because it's true – that you only live once, and I know that I'd far rather regret something I'd done than something I hadn't.

It was a great trip and I had an amazing time with my brother.

Ryan

At its inception, the Middle Kingdom Ride was purely and simply a way to spend some time with my brother and show him the China I've grown to love. Quite quickly, it became other things too – including a documentary film and a book that would enable us to share our experiences with other people, show them some of China's multitude of faces, and let them see what a great place it is for a motorcycle adventure.

On day 1, I was full of optimistic anticipation, as well as a certain amount of trepidation. So now I guess the question is: did I achieve what I set out to do? The answer in terms of meeting the challenge we'd set for ourselves is 'Yes'. As for blazing a trail for other people who want to ride motorcycles around China, I would have to say it's a fairly resounding 'Don't do it!'

China *is* a great place: the people are wonderful and the landscape is almost infinitely varied and spectacular. It's also a painfully difficult country to travel in if you want to go off the beaten track. The infrastructure is all there: there's a steadily expanding network of excellent expressways, but motorcyclists aren't allowed to use them, and some parts of the country are actually closed to foreigners.

I'd expected to have problems with the bikes; what I hadn't been prepared for were the unbendable, inexplicable, infuriating rules – although perhaps, having lived here for some time, I should have been. In some ways, I felt that China had let me down: I was disappointed to think that my brother's overriding impression might not be how incredible the country is, but how frustrating it is to do even the simplest thing here. It was a feeling that was colored, to some extent, by the problems inherent in finishing the trip on the east coast, where millions of people live, where there's a crazy amount of traffic on the roads, and where 'rules are rules', however ridiculous and illogical it is to enforce them in an individual case.

Colin and I went through so much together in those 65 days. We'd set ourselves a hugely difficult goal and we achieved it – and, in doing so, we created a powerful bond between us. We'd set the bar high in so many ways, and we rose to meet challenges that were far beyond anything we'd normally have to face in our everyday lives. It felt almost as though we'd been pitched against China and had come out on top.

We aren't professional motorcyclists; in fact, before we set out on the Middle Kingdom Ride, we were intermediate-level riders, without any particular skill or experience who'd learned most of what we knew during the short off-road Enduro course we did in Germany. We're not wealthy investment bankers or big-shot lawyers, we don't own major companies, and we weren't sponsored financially, so we had limited funds; and we're not celebrities on any list from A to Z. We're just two brothers who thought it would be cool to ride motorcycles around China.

It was probably just as well we didn't know when we set out just what we were letting ourselves in for. If we had, we might have missed the adventure of a lifetime, because, as well as the aggravations and disappointments, some very positive things came out of it all.

The Middle Kingdom Ride changed my life and my brother's life profoundly and forever. We learned a great deal about China; perhaps we learned even more about ourselves. I don't think any challenge we set ourselves in the future could be harder than the one we've already faced, and that gives me a tremendous sense of confidence and competence that will color every aspect of my life.

I shared the China I knew with my brother and discovered with him parts I didn't know. It would be great to feel that we'd been able to share China with other people too – with motorcycle riders, China lovers, and people who sit at desks in offices all around the world dreaming about having a truly life-changing adventure. Although I've said, 'Thinking of riding a motorcycle around China? Don't!' my message to those people is still, 'Follow your dreams – as Colin and I did – and don't let anything or anyone stop you.'

On Saturday, 14 August 2010, I left my house in Shanghai with tears in my eyes because I was saying goodbye to my family. By the time I arrived home again, 65 days later, I understood the value of everything I'd left behind me that day.

Acknowledgments

We owe a great deal to all the people who made The Middle Kingdom Ride possible and to those who have helped and supported us in other ways.

The MKRIDE team
Chad Ingraham, Jane Smith, Ted Hurley, Abdul, Kalsang, Kyle Murdoch, John Crawford, Yuan Yuan Wang, Jon Hogan.

The wonderful people who helped along the way
Andreas Wolf, Leo Xiao, Andreas Knapp (China Biker), Wenjie Li, Jeffrey Parker, Tim Sarch, Graham Allen, Lost Rider (ADV Rider Blogger), Mark Aitcheson, Andreas Quade, Andrew Kay.

Our corporate partners
Mandarin House Language School: Jasmine Bian.
Touratech: Herbert Schwarz, Margit Rowley, Karin Birkel.
Tomson Group: Charles Tong, Runa Zhou.
Cardo Systems: Michael Goren.
Oakley: Joe Cheung.
Kodak: Audrey Jonckheer.
Lowepro: Yvonne Petro, Kathy Campbell.
Pelican Products: Irina Obrzhutovich, Marcus Smith.
Airhawk: Steve Peyton, Rebecca Heckert.

2 brothers - 2 bikes -

18,000km

around China

www.mkride.com

facebook.com/mkride

2 brothers - 2 bikes -

14,000km

around India

www.TheIndiaRide.com

facebook.com/TheIndiaRide